The **Power** of
Stay Interviews
FOR **ENGAGEMENT** AND **RETENTION**

D0837752

The Power of
Stay Interviews

FOR ENGAGEMENT AND RETENTION

RICHARD P. FINNEGAN

Society for Human Resource Management
Alexandria, Virginia
www.shrm.org

Strategic Human Resource Management India
Mumbai, India
www.shrmindia.org

Society for Human Resource Management
Haidian District Beijing, China
www.shrm.org/cn

The Society for Human Resource Management (SHRM) is the world's largest association devoted to human resource management. Representing more than 250,000 members in over 140 countries, the Society serves the needs of HR professionals and advances the interests of the HR profession. Founded in 1948, SHRM has more than 575 affiliated chapters within the United States and subsidiary offices in China and India. Visit SHRM Online at www.shrm.org.

Interior and Cover Design: Terry Biddle

Library of Congress Cataloging-in-Publication Data

Finnegan, Richard P., 1950-
  The power of stay interviews for engagement and retention / Richard P. Finnegan. -- 1st ed.
     p. cm.
  Includes bibliographical references and index.
  ISBN 978-1-58644-234-7
  1. Employee attitude surveys. 2. Employee retention. I. Title.
  HF5549.5.A83F56 2011
  658.3'14--dc23
2011022097

11-0235

Contents

The 100-Word Introduction: This Book Is Right for You If vii

Chapter 1 | Making the Case: Why Stay Interviews Are Better 1

Chapter 2 | The Rethinking Retention Model® 9

Chapter 3 | Supervisors' Mighty Power to Drive Engagement and Retention 15

Chapter 4 | Stay Interview Essential Ingredients 25

Chapter 5 | Thinking Through Stay Interview Solutions 41

Chapter 6 | Three-Legged Power: Integrating Stay Interviews, Exit Surveys,
 and Employee Surveys 49

Chapter 7 | The Stay Interview Game 63

Chapter 8 | True Stories of Stay Interviews at Work 95

Chapter 9 | 'I've Burned the Ships' 105

Endnotes 109

Index 113

Interested in Learning More About Stay Interviews? 117

About the Author 119

Additional SHRM-Published Books 121

The 100-Word Introduction: This Book Is Right for You If ...

You feel like a hamster on a wheel regarding employee surveys that lead to the "same old" solutions.

Exit surveys say employees leave because of "jerk bosses" or for "better opportunities," and few outside human resources care.

You believe supervisors have immense power over employees' decisions to stay or leave ... and whether they work hard or easy ... but some supervisors "just don't get it."

The right data would convince executives if you could just put your hands on the right numbers.

You will take a strong position on HR's versus managers' roles regarding engagement and retention because winning is a team game.

You said "that's me" more than once, enjoy reading on.

Chapter 1 | Making the Case: Why Stay Interviews Are Better

For decades, organizations have struggled to find clear solutions to better engage and retain their best employees. At some point does it make sense to say, "Why don't we just ask them?"

Well, we *do* ask them. We ask them through engagement surveys, opinion surveys, climate surveys, and exit surveys. We survey online, over the phone, and with live and recorded voices. These surveys generate reports, and from reports come scores and rank orders, which then become benchmarks. From benchmarks we set goals to improve our scores on the next survey.

The primary outcome of all our surveys is *we build programs*. To improve recognition we add employee appreciation week and employee of the month. To improve communications we hold town hall meetings and write more informative newsletters. To improve careers we hold brown bag lunches and career fairs.

Our client executives tell us this ongoing survey process is like a hamster on a wheel. In the beginning, utilizing expanding technologies to measure employees' opinions as a pathway to improving them made sense. But over time these surveys have morphed into redundant administrative processes that effect few new outcomes. Instead they have become periodic rituals like preparing budgets, leading to jaded comments like "Is it that time again?"

The good news is that we have a better way to strengthen each employee's engagement and retention, and that better way is *simple*.

The Good and Bad News about Surveys

Let us look at the ways companies use employee surveys and examine what works and what does not work.

Exit surveys can be called the original retention tool. We have long believed that knowing why employees leave will direct us to retention solutions for survivors. But while based on logical thinking, exit surveys rarely lead to retention or engagement solutions. The primary obstacles are the following:

- Leaving employees often do not tell the truth.

- Employee participation is too low in part because surveys are too long.

- Surveys are designed to accept "attendance" and "better opportunity" as reasons for leaving, which fail to trigger solutions.

- Companies are reluctant to make policy or management changes based on "autopsies," on the words of employees who no longer work there.

Over the last few years, I have polled hundreds of HR professionals to determine if they had ever improved their companies based on exit survey results. The number who indicated they had improved their companies in any way was zero.[1]

The belief that exit surveys are a must-have tool has been reinforced by vendors that have leveraged technology to make gathering survey data easier for HR executives. Companies now purchase electronically delivered exit surveys that lead to pages of reports telling us how leavers rated their pay, benefits, communications, and other variables. Missing too often is learning *why the employee left*, although there is no guarantee that executives could improve their companies if they actually knew (see Table 1.1).

Table 1.1 | Exit Surveys vs. Stay Interviews	
Basically "autopsies" but not as scientific	Focuses on the current employees we want to keep
Departing employees won't burn bridges; often hide *real* reasons	Removes the "middle man" so leaders hear directly how to keep employees
Citing "better opportunity" or "attendance" as reasons to leave offers no real solutions	Employees hear: *We Want You To Stay*
HR managers say nothing gets done with results	Next steps are in supervisors' hands vs. program solutions

Various types of employee surveys have offered hope too. Learning how employees feel about a number of key items makes sense and will provide clues about what improvements companies must make to retain and engage them. And vendors have made surveying an easy process for companies to gather data and distribute reports.

These surveys provide value by supplying companies with benchmark data for internal and external comparisons, and they also offer rank-order scores for managers' effectiveness at supervising their teams. While providing data is their strength, detailing real engagement and retention solutions is their shortcoming (see Table 1.2).

Table 1.2 | Employee Surveys vs. Stay Interviews	
Present "average thinking" without learning top performers' needs	Supervisor hears why each individual employee stays and considers leaving
Usually ask for opinions but not importance so we won't know which items impact engagement or retention	Employee's priorities are clear and understood
Months pass before employee's opinions are communicated and acted on	Interview and solutions happen quickly, in real time
Lead to action plans with more program vs. better 1:1 supervision	Next steps are in the hands of supervisors who are responsible for engagement and retention

Again, the dilemma with this approach is that *all solutions are programs*. By their nature, employee surveys are confidential, so you do not know what your best performers think, and all data represents *average thinking*. Further, survey results typically report all items as equal in importance for driving retention and engagement, whether your survey includes 12 items or 70. The result is that managers focus on driving up lower scores without knowing if those lower scores represent items employees care most about. And the solutions they provide touch all employees in the same way, regardless of the unique needs of each employee.

One way to measure the effectiveness of employee surveys is to ask, "Will our resulting action plan lead to improved engagement and retention for our top performers?" The real answer is you just don't know.

The Stay Interview Advantage

A Stay Interview is a structured discussion a leader conducts with each individual employee to learn the specific actions he or she must take to strengthen that employee's engagement and retention with the organization.

Stay Interviews do three things that surveys do not. They bring information that can be used *today*; they give insights for engaging and retaining *individual employees* including top performers; and they put *managers* in the solution seat for developing individual stay plans. Gone are the following obstacles and distractions from implementing real engagement and retention solutions:

- **Time delays.** Delays occur from surveying employees to distributing reports to writing action plans to implementing those actions. How soon does data become stale?

- **Watered-down solutions.** Since all data is aggregated into groups, only group fixes can be developed which paint all employees with one brush regardless of whether they are your best or worst performers.

- **Short-term, feel-good programs.** Perks like casual Fridays or free coffee check the box for new initiatives but do nothing to improve supervisory skills, and ultimately have no bearing on whether employees stay or leave or increase their engagement.

How much can your company improve engagement and retention with programs alone, without effective day-to-day supervision and leadership? When is the last time you heard a good employee say, *"My boss treats me like dirt, but I'm holding out for employee appreciation week. I'll get a balloon and a hot dog, and I'll be re-stoked for another 52 weeks"*?

Leaders who substitute programs for fine-tuned supervision skills take few steps if any toward actually becoming better leaders.

What Are 'Engagement' and 'Retention'? And How Much Are They Really Worth?

Here are our definitions for engagement and retention as we refer to them throughout this book:

- **Engagement:** *Employees are fully committed each day to giving their all to help their organizations succeed.*
- **Retention:** *Those employees the organization wants to keep stay with their organizations.*

Our definitions are pure and deliberately simple: *Employees who give their best each day, and they stay.* Disengagement then means companies having employees who underperform, and turnover refers to companies losing employees they wish to keep. We recognize that good employees sometimes leave for reasons beyond their organizations' control and that many examples of turnover do indeed create healthy opportunities for others. But our fundamental approach is that organizations want all employees to be fully engaged and that they also wish to keep all employees they *want* to keep.

Disengagement and turnover are extraordinarily expensive. A Watson Wyatt study tells us that a one standard deviation improvement in engagement is associated with a 1.9 percent increase in revenue per employee.[1] To put this amount into perspective, typical employees in the study's sample work at firms where productivity equals about $250,000 per employee, meaning that a significant improvement in engagement is associated with an increase in revenue per employee of $4,675. For a typical S&P 500 organization, this amount represents a revenue increase of $93.5 million. And the proportional increase is just as large for small- and medium-sized companies.[2]

Regarding turnover, the Saratoga Institute tells us that turnover costs organizations over 12 percent of pretax income, up to 40 percent for some.[3] Another study indicates that turnover across the U.S. costs $25 billion annually, just to train replacements.[4] A third study tells us that turnover reduces U.S. corporate earnings and stock prices by 38 percent in four high-turnover industries.[5]

So finding *real solutions* to engagement and retention is essential for corporate success.

Chapter 2 | The Rethinking Retention Model®

I n my previous book, *Rethinking Retention in Good Times and Bad*, I presented the first-ever comprehensive model for employee retention.[1] This model is based on research in that each solution has worked consistently to improve retention in organizations, and respected academic and professional studies have proved the value of many of these solutions. The model is also based on *processes*, as it is accompanied by tactical solutions that must be implemented and kept in place forever in order for these processes to work best.

Figure 2.1 depicts The Rethinking Retention Model.

The "elevator speech" for the model is that employee retention is a shared responsibility for human resources and line managers, and that solving turnover with programs alone is at best a partial solution. This is no slight whatsoever to HR professionals who every day invent creative, effective ways to connect employees to their organizations. However, the role of first-line supervisors in retention is so powerful that HR managers can only be

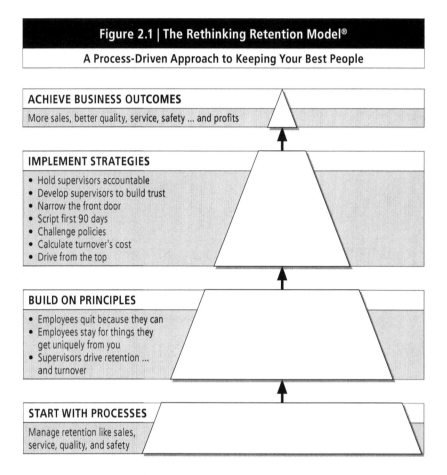

Figure 2.1 | The Rethinking Retention Model®

A Process-Driven Approach to Keeping Your Best People

ACHIEVE BUSINESS OUTCOMES

More sales, better quality, service, safety ... and profits

IMPLEMENT STRATEGIES

- Hold supervisors accountable
- Develop supervisors to build trust
- Narrow the front door
- Script first 90 days
- Challenge policies
- Calculate turnover's cost
- Drive from the top

BUILD ON PRINCIPLES

- Employees quit because they can
- Employees stay for things they get uniquely from you
- Supervisors drive retention ... and turnover

START WITH PROCESSES

Manage retention like sales, service, quality, and safety

held responsible for retaining the employees who work in human resources.

The model also describes where human resources can make its best contributions. Let us take a closer look at the principles and strategies.

The Principles at the Foundation of Retention

1. **Employees quit jobs because they can.** Workplace demographics leave high-performing employees with

too many job choices, even in down economies. Avoid the dead-end road of basing retention solutions on exit surveys and other reasons you believe employees leave. Instead, build a proactive solution you can control.

2. **Employees stay for things they get uniquely from you.** Who are you as an employer? What does your organization offer that others do not? How do you know why each individual employee stays, including your top performers? Build hiring, training, and all other processes on the things that are uniquely you.

3. **Supervisors build unique relationships that drive retention ... or turnover.** Supervisory relationships are one-of-a-kind levers that deeply impact employees' stay/leave decisions. Some employees stay for supervisors; some leave because of them; and some are indifferent to them.

The Strategies of the Rethinking Retention Model

4. **Hold supervisors accountable for achieving retention goals.** Supervisors will not achieve any other goal you assign them if they lose their best or even good performers, so make them accountable and give them "skin in the game" for increasing retention.

5. **Develop supervisors to build trust with their teams.** Communication, recognition, and development all fall behind trust. Who values information and praise if you do not believe it? Employees cannot trust jerk bosses and the definition of jerk bosses is those you cannot trust.

6. **Narrow the front door to close the back door.** New hires must align with who you are, accept doing the

worst aspects of your jobs, and give clear indications they intend to stay.

7. **Script employees' first 90 days.** Supervisors must know historic tipping points for how long new hires should stay before the initial turnover surge has passed. What built-in connection points do you have for new employees after onboarding and training?

8. **Challenge policies to ensure they drive retention.** Discard last decade's thinking, and drive your rules toward retention. The best solution to work/life balance is schedule and work style flexibility.

9. **Calculate turnover's cost to galvanize retention as a business issue.** Dollars speak louder than numbers and percents and must be tied to retention goal achievement.

10. **Drive retention from the top** because executives have the greatest impact on achieving retention goals.

Compare your company's approach toward retention to its ways for improving sales, service, quality, or safety. In most organizations, sales are driven from the CEO down to sales managers and salespersons with clear goals, accountabilities, and consequences, both good and bad. The line or operating side of the organization accepts full responsibility for sales outcomes and looks to staff support departments for help with sales training, sales tracking, sales promotions, and the formation of sales awards. When sales goals are exceeded, sales managers and their teams win trips to Hawaii, and few send postcards to their helpers in staff support departments.

This is as it should be, except for the postcards, because consequences work both ways for those who actually sell. Similar consequences must be in place for those who are responsible for engaging and retaining their teams.

The point is that companies struggle with where to place accountability for retention and usually miss the mark. In research asking if managers are held accountable for achieving retention goals, one study reported 14 percent of companies had installed such accountabilities, and another study reported just 11 percent.[2] And these "accountabilities" probably took many forms, from clearly established goals with consequences to references about employee retention in the talent management section of performance appraisal forms.

This absence of accountability happens at the top of organizations as well as in the middle. We recently completed a research study with ExecuNet and found that only 6 percent of CEOs indicated that their pay or bonus is directly hit when they lose a key executive.[3]

Figure 2.2 asks whether your organization approaches retention as *process-driven by leaders* or as *program-driven by human resources*. The Rethinking Retention Model® makes clear that both sides must play key roles in retention and that line leaders must accept and be held accountable to

Figure 2.2 | Process or Program-Driven?

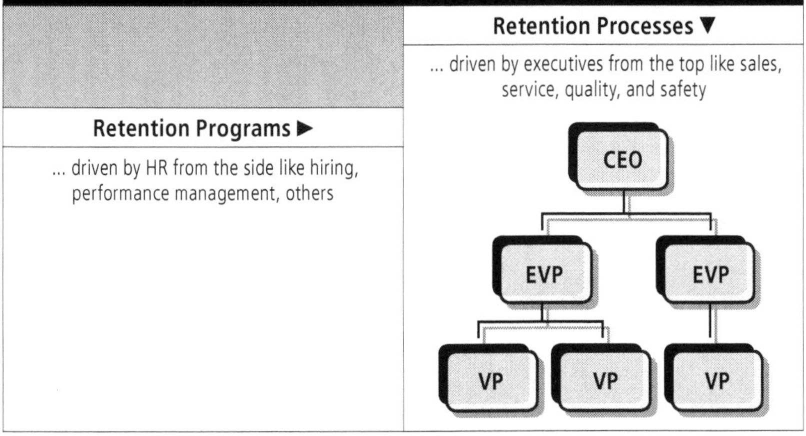

Retention Processes ▼
... driven by executives from the top like sales, service, quality, and safety

Retention Programs ▶
... driven by HR from the side like hiring, performance management, others

employee retention goals ... just as they are held accountable for sales, service, quality, and safety.

A large volume of research affirms that the Rethinking Retention Model® is valid. Stay Interviews, then, produce synchronized connections with four parts on the Model as these points are described on pages 10 to 12:

Point #2: Employees stay for things they get uniquely from you.

Point #3: Supervisors build unique relationships that drive retention ... or turnover.

Point #4: Hold supervisors accountable for achieving retention goals.

Point #5: Develop supervisors to build trust with their teams.

Stay Interviews become important if not essential tools to help supervisors achieve their retention goals. They empower leaders on all levels to move from implementing one-size-fits-all programs to building focused, one-on-one retention plans with each employee. The leader's role is then clearly stated — to make the plan succeed and to retain the employee — all while deepening engagement and gaining the added productivity that results.

Chapter 3 | Supervisors' Mighty Power to Drive Engagement and Retention

Most of you who read this book already "get it" regarding the impact of the supervisor-employee relationship on engagement and retention. You have learned this from your own personal experiences at work as well as by observing the outcomes that high-performing supervisors bring to your organization. But let us take a look at relevant research in this area to strengthen our beliefs and, if necessary, to convince others.

As we study the following data, let us draw a clear boundary between the impact *leaders* have on engagement versus the impact well-designed and well-meaning *employee programs* have on engagement. "Leaders" in this context means supervisors on each level from CEOs down to first-line leaders. "Programs" refers to one-size-fits-all initiatives that are intended to improve engagement and employee morale. While the impact of leaders and programs is sometimes hard to separate, there is convincing data that *the relationships leaders form with their teams is directly related to those teams' levels of engagement.*

A study by Development Dimensions International (DDI) found that "engagement is strongly influenced by leadership quality" and that employees' levels of engagement were considerably higher when their supervisors had higher levels of engagement as well.[1] DDI also found that employees who report to highly engaged supervisors were less likely to indicate they may leave the organization within a year. More compelling are the six personal characteristics DDI identified as closely linked to engagement. As you read these characteristics, consider whether employees are likely to improve in these areas as a result of one-size-fits-all programs designed to accommodate everyone:

- **Adaptability.** Openness to new ideas and experiences; readily modifying work approaches in response to change

- **Achievement orientation.** Pushing oneself through a continual cycle of setting goals, reaching them, and setting progressively more challenging goals

- **Attraction to work.** Maintaining a positive view of one's job despite periods of stress and frustration

- **Emotional maturity.** Avoiding impulsive actions and extreme or sustained emotional reactions that would negatively impact work effectiveness and co-worker relations

- **Positive disposition.** Demonstrating agreeableness with customers and peers; eagerness to help others accomplish work goals

- **Self-efficacy.** Exhibiting secure, unyielding confidence in the ability to succeed in the job and to advance beyond one's current position

Supervisors' pathways for developing these characteristics involve providing feedback, coaching, and developing positive one-on-one relationships versus instituting program fixes.

Another study takes us in this same direction but adds a new twist. In this research, titled *The Power of Federal Employee Engagement*, the U.S. Merit Systems Protection Board reports, "Even a cursory review of the 16 questions that we used to measure employee engagement reveals how important supervisors are to their subordinates' level of engagement."[2] The report then lists a sample of question areas from an engagement scale labeled "supervisors have a major influence." Here is the list:

- Communicating job expectations
- Making good use of employees' skills and abilities
- Ensuring that employees have the resources to do their jobs well
- Providing employees with challenging assignments
- Rewarding and recognizing employees appropriately
- Giving employees an opportunity to improve their skills
- Treating employees with respect
- Valuing employee opinions
- Fostering an environment of cooperation and teamwork

This study further drives home the power of supervisors on engagement by asking both engaged and disengaged employees if their supervisors had "good management skills." Of the employees who were engaged, 87 percent agreed that their supervisors had good management skills. Conversely, of the employees who were not engaged, a mere 13.7 percent agreed that their supervisors had good management skills.

Gallup provides us with a third view on supervisors' impact on engagement. In its study titled "Feeling Good Matters in the Workplace," Gallup categorized employees as either engaged, not engaged, or actively disengaged.[3] The survey states that "supervisors play a crucial role in engagement" and then provides supportive data from three survey items … whether supervisors focus on strengths or on positive characteristics, employees' interactions with co-workers, and whether employees feel challenged.

Research led by the American Society for Training and Development (ASTD) provides us with an additional perspective on leaders and engagement. In "Learning's Role in Employee Engagement," just 15 percent of respondents agree to a high or very high extent that their leaders are skilled at engaging the workforce.[4] The study concludes, "The bottom line is that many leaders and managers need considerably better engagement-building skills than they currently have."

Concluding that supervisors have a strong impact on engagement is clear and easy. The crucial question for our discussion is *how effectively can supervisors improve engagement with one-size-fits-all programs*, and the answer is *not very well*.

How Important Are Supervisors for Retention?

For most of us, the link between leaders and retention is intuitive, just as it is for engagement. The supportive data is overwhelming, and it too spotlights the production power that results from leaders on all levels *developing relationships with their teams via skills versus programs*. Let us look at just a few of the available studies.

The Saratoga Institute found that poor leadership causes over 60 percent of all employee turnover.[5] Its study was extensive, covering more than 19,000 employees across 17 industry groups, and specified that the majority leave because they are not recognized or not coached by their supervisors.

Gallup consultants Marcus Buckingham and Curt Coffman disclosed in *First, Break All the Rules*, "If you have a turnover problem, look first to your managers."[6] They go on to say that "how long that employee stays and how productive he is ... is determined by his relationship with his immediate supervisor." These conclusions are based on study results from over one million employees and 80,000 managers, compiled over a period of 25 years.

A Kenexa study adds new flavor to the relationship between supervisors and retention.[7] Kenexa surveyed employees who had left organizations and asked about their fit with supervisors as well as their satisfaction with pay, benefits, learning, development, and advancement. In all instances, employees' opinions were "mediated," or influenced by relationships these employees had with their supervisors. The study concludes with:

> *Offering a higher salary or developmental/advancement opportunities may not be enough to retain employees.*

So how do the results of this study differ from the other studies? In Figure 3.1, we depict the typical assumption that employees' engagement and retention are influenced by factors that are delivered by two distinct sources: *supervision* from their leader and *programs* from human resources. But the Kenexa results paint a very different picture, that employees see these factors as ultimately being delivered via one primary source: their leader, as shown in Figure 3.2.

Figure 3.1 | We Think Employees View Key Aspects of Work Regardless of How They View Their Supervisors ...

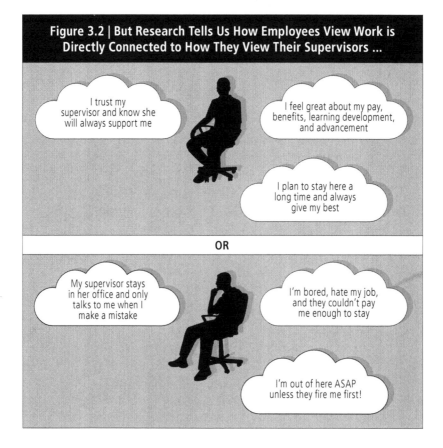

Figure 3.2 | But Research Tells Us How Employees View Work is Directly Connected to How They View Their Supervisors ...

This study more than any other we know highlights the upside and downside potential of supervisors' impact on their teams, as it tells us that *how employees view their supervisor impacts how they view everything about their employment relationship*. Let us consider supervisors as all-inclusive ports through which employees receive and filter everything you offer as an organization. This thinking then takes us to the following two equations:

Strong Supervision + Effective Employee Programs = High Employee Retention

Weak Supervision + Effective Employee Programs = High Employee Turnover

Other studies tell us that this same link between supervisors and retention happens globally, regardless of native culture. Also, specific research points out that supervisors have a strong influence on stay and leave decisions with nurses and teachers, representing jobs that we usually associate only with the rigors of their duties or perceived low pay.

The easy analysis for whether supervisors can improve retention with programs alone is to compare peer retention rates over time. Where peer supervisors manage the same types of employees with the same pay, benefits, training, and supportive programs, you should assume these programs are dominant factors in stay/leave decisions only *if retention rates are similar for all supervisors*. But if peer supervisor retention rates are significantly different, employees likely choose to stay for those supervisors with the best relationship-building skills.

Supervisors' Roles in Building Trust

It is easy to view trust as intangible, as a quality that is in the air between two people that somehow affects their relationship. Research, though, tells us that *trust between each supervisor and his or her individual employees is the absolute most important ingredient for building loyalty and engagement*.

Leadership IQ found that a full 32 percent of employees' decisions to stay with their companies were based on how much these employees trusted their supervisors.[8] Walker Information found that employees' loyalty was most influenced by their perceptions of fairness, care and concern, and trust at work.[9]

Perhaps the loudest declaration of the power of trust is presented by the Great Place to Work Institute. The Institute is the engine behind the *Fortune* 100 Best Places to Work For, and the results of its survey count as two-thirds of each applicant company's overall ranking. The Institute's primary belief is stated this way: "Our 20 years of research have proven that trust between managers and employees is the defining primary characteristic of the very best workplaces."[10]

Note that the reference is to trust "between managers and employees" versus alluding to trust in more general terms such as a desirable organizational characteristic between employees and executives. This distinction is because trust between supervisors and employees is *personal*, based on daily interactions that drive how employees view their worth at work and maybe how they view themselves at a far deeper level. Employees have super-strong, always-present feelings about how much their supervisors are looking out for them and truly want them to succeed. Less meaningful is whether supervisors tell them they did a good job or give them feedback on performance. The result is that to a significant degree employees measure their companies based on how much they trust their supervisors.

Here is one way to appreciate the power of trust, formed as a bet. Think about the best supervisor you ever had, and now compare that supervisor to the worst supervisor you ever had. I will wager $5 that you trusted your best supervisor and did not trust your worst one. And another $5 that your best supervisor had weaknesses you easily overlooked and that your worst supervisor had strengths you could not see.

Here is a way to drive home the power of trust to managers, too. Ask them to recall the most damaging trust-breaking experience of their careers and describe how it made them *feel* and how it made them *change*. Then once they have revisited these painful times and have fully absorbed their emotions and outcomes, ask them if any of their current or former employees might be thinking of *them* when doing this exercise.

This experience illustrates two salient points: (1) that being on the receiving end of broken trust is painful and potentially career-changing and (2) that all of us are subject to breaking trust *because doing so is about behaviors rather than about character*. And *all of us* behave incorrectly at times, and *all of us* can change those habits.

Google's Quest to Build a Better Boss

A recent study by Google, about Google, summarizes the power of first-line supervisors. Google conducted an extensive, inside look at what made their best bosses the best by consulting various forms of employee data. The result underscored the power of conducting one-on-one meetings with employees to help them grow.

Laszlo Bock, Google's vice president for people operations, explained that in the past Google's management approach was to "leave people alone ... if they become stuck they will ask their bosses." The study, though, found that technical skills such as writing code was dead last on the priorities of Google's best bosses. The most important skill for the best bosses was described this way:

> "What employees valued most were even-keeled bosses who made time for one-on-one meetings, who helped people puzzle through problems by asking questions, not dictating answers, and who took an interest in employees' lives and careers."

This study, along with other data presented above, make clear that managers on all levels who do not invest the time to connect with employees individually to better understand their jobs, careers, and life needs are not operating at full capacity.[11]

Chapter 4 | Stay Interview Essential Ingredients

I n this chapter we will examine the basic parts of Stay Interviews that must be in place in order for supervisors on all levels to use them most effectively. Before moving forward, let us consider a few of the hidden advantages Stay Interviews offer that can easily slip through the cracks:

- **Employees hear directly from their supervisors that they care and that they wish them to stay and grow with the company.** The supervisor/employee bond is critical to improving engagement and retention, and supervisors deliver clear messages during the Stay Interviews that each employee is instrumental in achieving the company's success and that supervisors want them to stay.

- **Supervisors further accept retention and engagement within their sphere of responsibility.** Combining Stay Interviews with retention goals and other initiatives results in a clear understanding that responsibility for retention and engagement lies with individual supervisors who are in the best position to influence and drive improvements.

- **Employees are more likely to accept responsibility for staying.** Stay Interviews require supervisors to ask, listen, consider, and then follow-up on employees' requests. This responsibility builds a new form of glue that causes employees not only to stay longer but also to proactively approach their supervisors with a future concern before looking for another job.

- **Stay Interviews build trust.** Supervisors who ask, listen, act, and communicate honestly strengthen trust with their employees, the absolutely most valuable supervisory skill for increasing engagement and retention.

Think of Stay Interviews as having the following components in Figure 4.1.

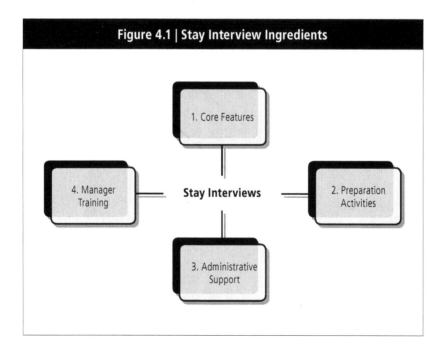

Figure 4.1 | Stay Interview Ingredients

Core Features

Let us revisit the Stay Interview definition:

> *A Stay Interview is a structured discussion a leader conducts with each individual employee to learn the specific actions that leader must take to strengthen the employee's engagement and retention with the organization.*

So core features include that *leaders* conduct Stay Interviews. "Leaders" is defined here as anyone who manages someone, so this term may be synonymous in your organization with executives, managers, supervisors, or leads. These terms are also substituted for each other throughout this book.

Human resources at times may be called on to conduct Stay Interviews for employees who work outside human resources, but this situation should occur in exceptional circumstances only. Best outcomes will happen when leaders are in the Stay Interview chair and hear directly from their employees about how they wish to be managed for better engagement and retention. "I'm too busy" is not a legitimate reason for managers to ask human resources to conduct Stay Interviews.

The definition also indicates that leaders should conduct Stay Interviews individually, one-on-one. While conducting Stay Interviews in small groups is certainly more efficient, some employees will contribute less in public. Leaders will also face an easy temptation to design group solutions versus individual solutions, which then become programs rather than customized stay plans for individual employees.

Here are other core features of Stay Interviews:

- **Cascade:** The first Stay Interviews should be conducted by the top executive of the company or unit with his or her direct reports, and then the interviews should cascade down throughout the rest of the team to first-line supervisors with their direct reports. All leaders, except the top executive, should first experience a Stay Interview as an employee. This means that each leader's Stay Interview performance becomes a role model for each of his or her subordinate leaders, and those subordinate leaders will likely manage their Stay Interviews with their teams in the same ways that their leader did.

- **In person:** Stay Interviews should ideally be conducted in person rather than remotely whenever possible, even if the meeting must be scheduled months in advance due to travel or some form of telecommuting.

- **Setting expectations:** Leaders should tell teams in advance that they will schedule individual Stay Interviews with employees to learn what the leader can do to help employees stay longer and to feel fully engaged in their work. The leader should also emphasize that the focus will be on matters he or she can influence or control rather than on issues that relate to broader company policies, but the leader will listen to all employee questions or concerns.

- **Scheduling:** Most Stay Interviews take 20 minutes or less to conduct, but some will carry on longer. Leaders should consider telling employees to allow 20 minutes for their meeting, but leaders should then allow 30 minutes on their calendars. Also, leaders should schedule an "easy" meeting first to build confidence in their skills and in the process and then move on to employees who are most important to engage and keep, followed by the rest.

- **Separate from performance:** Stay Interviews should focus on identifying specific improvements that raise the employee's levels of engagement and retention and should not morph into ways the employee can perform better. Thus, Stay Interviews should not be add-ons to performance appraisal meetings but be separate meetings that are entirely focused on what each leader can do for the employee.

- **Scripted openings:** Leaders must open meetings with scripts that both point the employee in the right direction and avoid any appearance of an implied contract. Here are some examples:

  » "I'd like our focus to be on subjects I can help you with each day," in contrast to suggesting that the meeting is specifically to discuss pay, benefits, or company direction, although these may become topics that need to be addressed.

  » "My hope is that we can work together for a long time" is safe of any implied commitments found in statements such as "I'm sure we'll always have a job for you, given your performance."

  » And if needed, "I know you are having some performance struggles, but I'm hopeful you can improve them" is a way of acknowledging performance problems but then moving past them since the Stay Interview may unlock issues that contribute to the employee's performance problems.

Preparation Activities

Here are suggestions for getting your Stay Interviews off to a great start.

Recommended Questions

These questions should be open-ended and can cover basic issues as well as any that are relevant to your company. What do you like most and least about working here?

What are your career goals? Your dream job? Why do you stay? Why might you leave? What makes a good day here? What more do you want to learn? How can I help? While some questions should be scripted, leaders should know that probing is essential and can result in questions not in the script.

Target Audience

While most companies schedule Stay Interviews for all employees, you may want to start with one department that faces uphill challenges on engagement or retention. Other targeted groups could include employees in positions with high turnover, those who have reached a certain length of service that tends to trigger turnover based on past turnover data, or those from a unit that has recently suffered from job cuts resulting in more work for survivors. Another targeted group may be older employees who are eligible to retire but whom you want to stay.

Gaining support across the entire company for a major initiative can be difficult, so another targeted group may be a team whose leader will go first and carry out Stay Interviews with high energy. That leader can then broadcast the results to peer leaders so the project spreads across the entire organization.

High Performers

Many of your best performers take regular calls from headhunters and have never-ending opportunities to leave. Deepening their engagement and retention is more critical than doing the same for those who perform their jobs less effectively, so you may consider conducting their Stay Interviews first or initially narrowing the Stay Interview project to only this group.

But consider, too, that strengthening engagement and retention for all employees who perform their jobs in satisfactory ways is essential.

Schedule

Conducting Stay Interviews must be tied to a predetermined schedule in order to be effective. Unlike other management tasks, the cascading nature of Stay Interviews means that if one leader falls behind, all leaders below that leader must wait and potentially move back their appointments with their teams. A smart move would be to identify those leaders who are typically late conducting performance appraisals and to advise them that doing Stay Interviews late has even greater consequences because it negatively impacts large groups beneath them ... and their lateness will be visible to others.

Scripted Responses

Leaders must know how to respond to employee concerns that have no easy answers. Examples include an employee who performs his or her job adequately and wants an immediate pay increase or an employee in a 7-day operation who wants off work on weekends and holidays. Others might ask for smaller health care premiums. These types of issues are usually out of the immediate supervisors' control, and some of these requests will never be met. So leaders must have scripts on how to handle them.

Solutions

Leaders must know how to respond to complex issues they can address, too. These may include career plans, training opportunities, customized pay plans, flexible schedules, or other possible but complex requests. Leaders should be especially attuned to the needs of high performers whose contributions are difficult and expensive to replace.

The primary counsel to give leaders regarding solutions is for them to feel comfortable raising the stop sign and scheduling a second meeting with the employee. The leader can then consult with his or her manager or with human resources to get additional ideas for that employee's stay plan. More information on solutions is included later in this book.

Large Spans of Control

Decide in advance the best plans for leaders who have high numbers of direct reports to complete their Stay Interviews in a reasonable period of time. These discussions sometimes lead to discoveries about the roles of "leads" and employees with similar titles who guide the work of others but who have limited supervisory authority. In some cases, employees see leads as their actual supervisors; therefore, the leads are the appropriate ones to conduct the Stay Interviews, after training of course. For those leaders with a large staff who have no help, ask them to schedule several Stay Interviews each week until all are completed.

Follow-Up Frequency

Leaders should be given a timeline for following up with their employees on the success of their individualized stay plans. Frequency can be consistent for all, such as every 90 days, or can vary based on the complexity of each stay plan. For example, leaders would want to follow up frequently with a high performer who is working toward a specific certification or on an internal development plan. But that same leader may not meet as frequently with employees who perform their jobs adequately and are pleased with their current roles.

Stay Interview Frequency

Leaders should conduct Stay Interviews with all employees at least annually and in some cases more frequently if engagement or retention is an especially high concern. New hires should also benefit from Stay Interviews at about their 90th day of employment or earlier if turnover is peaking shortly after hire. Organizations may schedule ongoing Stay Interviews for one year from the same month as the initial Stay Interview, and then continue on that same-month yearly schedule. Another way is to schedule Stay Interviews six months after each performance review, in part to ensure the performance discussion and stay discussion are separate.

Administrative Support

Stay Interviews require support tools so leaders can proceed efficiently, consistently, and successfully. Each of the following tools should be considered for the value it brings.

Structured Interview Forms

The forms can include opening scripts, questions, possible probes following each question, and areas for notes. Providing this form to leaders will enable them to complete the Stay Interview process by remaining focused on their employees' words and overall content.

Stay Interview Plan Forms

These forms provide structure for leaders to write in actual steps they will take as a result of the interview. The form should also include an area for employee's responsibilities, as they must have accountabilities within their stay plans. Leaders can then share this document with their managers and with the employee and then update it periodically to track accomplishments.

Stay Interview Department Summaries

These forms provide summary information leaders learn from their teams such as the top three reasons employees stay and the top three reasons employees would leave. They can also include summary information on stay plans. Managers the next level up use this data to ensure stay plans are on track and to spot trends among their overall teams.

Stay Interview Company-Wide Summaries

These forms aggregate all information from the department summary forms to provide a comprehensive picture of all employees' stay reasons, potential leave reasons, and individualized stay plans. HR executives and others at the top of organizations benefit from these data because they provide insight into employee trends and can help direct future policy decisions. Analyzing data by specific jobs, length of service, and employee performance leads to deeper thinking about company-wide policies and programs to improve engagement and retention.

Manager Training

Managers must be trained on the reasons for conducting Stay Interviews, on the skills required for success, and on the processes used by your company. Below is a list of training topics you may want to include. If you have a designated training department, consider asking the employees there to help with program design and delivery.

Why Do Stay Interviews?

Consider sharing company or department turnover information, employee survey results, company mission and values statements, and any other information that supports your inviting leaders to invest the time required to train for and conduct Stay Interviews.

Why Us?

Leaders may wonder why they are being asked to take on this project that looks like "an HR assignment." Use data presented earlier in this book, as well as local stories and testimonies, to demonstrate the immense power leaders have on their teams' engagement and retention. Consider also discussing the power of leaders who build trust, and use the exercises mentioned earlier if helpful. For those who believe they do not have time, suggest they meet with their managers to arrange priorities.

Didn't We Just Do a Survey a Few Months Ago?

Explain the value of leaders developing individual stay plans for each member of their teams versus implementing programs that usually result from employee surveys. Emphasize that good employee programs can be effective, and cite a company-wide career or recognition program as an example. Then communicate the four benefits that Stay Interviews bring that employee surveys do not that are noted at the beginning of this chapter.

Won't This Lead to Disappointments?

Some leaders will immediately envision getting caught in a discussion about an especially uncomfortable topic like pay. Others may immediately think of that one team member who is always asking for more. Their essential thought will be, "Why stir things up when we can keep things quiet?"

Expect these feelings to be real for some, and approach them proactively. Tell them that the Stay Interview process leads to far more increases than decreases in engagement and retention and that they will be given scripts and help to resolve all employee requests.

What If Our Employees Don't Trust Us?

While few will openly ask this question, leaders will wonder if all employees will candidly disclose their thoughts rather than dodge weighty topics to escape the meeting. Explain that *conducting Stay Interviews is in itself a trust-building opportunity* and that each leader can build trust by taking notes, listening, probing, and following through on commitments. The solid measure is whether your team trusts you more *after* conducting Stay Interviews than before.

Your Stay Interview Process

Describe step-by-step how your Stay Interviews will work, including forms your leaders will use.

Stay Interview Skills

Provide instructions and exercises to teach the skills for conducting effective Stay Interviews. These skills should include the following:

- **Taking notes:** Doing so causes us to listen better and to maintain our focus, and it shows speakers that their words matter.

- **Listening:** Teaching leaders to repeat back what they hear is one easy technique for building their listening skills.

- **Probing for more information:** Phrases such as "Can you tell me more about that?," "Can you give me an example?," and "How important is this to you?" all open the door to finding the absolute best pathways to engagement and retention.

- **Developing effective stay plans:** Stay plans must be customized and on target, addressing each employee's most pressing issues with either a spot-on way for moving forward or a clear reason for saying no. Furthermore, leaders must find out and address *the chief issues* rather than bypass them for lack of an easy fix.

- **Taking responsibility for company policies:** Tough discussions about pay, schedules, and other sensitive topics lead some supervisors to dodge their responsibilities by pointing up the organization chart; doing so may feel good for the moment but sends clear messages that the leader sympathizes with the employee but has no power. Teach leaders to use first-person pronouns like "I" and "we" and avoid saying the ubiquitous "they" when referring to executives above them.

Role-Play an Effective Stay Interview

We all know employees cringe when hearing the "r word," but role plays are very effective teaching methods when facilitated correctly. These can be done live with prepared employee "actors" or demonstrated via a video that has been filmed in advance. Use these techniques to make the role play work best:

- Choose someone for the leader role who is likely to play both the verbal and nonverbal parts just right by taking notes, listening, and asking the best probing questions.

- Ask the person playing the employee to play *himself* or *herself* rather than make up a totally fictional role; doing so increases everyone's interest and leads to a more complex ... and real ... role play.

- Interrupt the role play at critical points to involve audience members; ask them what probes they would use or solutions they would recommend. Enhance their skills by asking them to convert their probe ideas into specific questions, or ask them to replace the leader in the role play so they ask their question directly to the "employee."

- Ask the "employee" to raise a controversial issue about pay, benefits, or schedules that leaders fear most; then ask the audience to role play ways to respond.

- Conclude the role play by asking the audience members what they saw and liked and would do differently; expect them to focus on the verbal parts of the interview, so bring them back to nonverbal aspects such as note-taking and listening.

Here is a true example of learning through role plays. We helped to implement Stay Interviews at Florida Hospital Flagler, and during the training the food services manager volunteered to play herself as the employee in the role play. When asked what her manager could do to make her work life better, the food services manager said she wanted to learn more about computers and also about international foods. We paused the role play and asked all the managers in the room for ideas for helping this employee enjoy her work more. Here is how the dialogue unfolded:

- The first manager to speak said she would show the food services manager how to locate international food sites on her computer.

- The second manager said she would teach her to set up these sites as "favorites," so they would be easily available to her.

- Then another manager said she would go to a book store and search for a food magazine with international recipes and buy it for her.

- This triggered another manager to say, "If you are buying her a magazine, why not get her a subscription? They're pretty cheap."

HR Director Alyson Parker concluded the idea-generating session by saying, "Ask her to have International Foods Day once each month in the hospital cafeteria, and then we'll all enjoy her work!"

This role play was about a real employee expressing ways she could become better engaged and retained. The group-solution exercise became an impromptu example of crowdsourcing, as all pitched in with good ideas that would for certain help the food services manager heighten her engagement and loyalty in real life.

Provide the Schedule

Describe the cascading schedule for the Stay Interview rollout, and emphasize that leaders on each level must make their deadlines.

'What Do I Do Next?'

Conclude the meeting by telling leaders that unless they are the CEO, the next thing they should do is nothing. They should wait until their manager schedules and conducts his or her own Stay Interview, and then follow the schedule by conducting Stay Interviews with their teams.

One Final Note about Training Managers

The top-down nature of Stay Interviews requires high-est executives to go first. Whether the top executive in your project is the CEO or a division manager, his or her performance will set the tone for others and become the model for how Stay Interviews will be conducted by all subordinate leaders down to the first-line supervisor lev-el. Offer these executives a one-on-one coaching session to build their skills, especially if they are unable to at-tend a training session. Do the same for others at the top if individual coaching will help them conduct their Stay Interviews more expertly.

Chapter 5 | Thinking Through Stay Interview Solutions

Imagine nirvana, that all your leaders completely understand the full range of developmental tools available to them. And while you are imagining, picture each leader conducting a comprehensive Stay Interview with each employee to put all issues on the table and addressing each issue in the best possible ways.

OK, snap out of it! Stay Interviews will not lead to perfect outcomes, but they will certainly improve engagement and retention in your company. And they will do this by helping your leaders foster more productive one-on-one relationships with their employees.

Preparing for Basic Q & A

Identify the top 5 to 10 issues that some employees will raise, and provide scripts to your leaders to give them comfort. Consider inviting a small group of leaders to offer input for the scripts so that the content rings true to them and their peers. Table 5.1 provides a broad-based sample of possible issues, and at least some of these will apply to your company.

Table 5.1 | Possible Issues Employees May Raise
1. What can I do to get out of working weekends?
2. I'd like more input into company and department decisions.
3. I can't live on my pay and I need a big raise.
4. I'm bored and need to do something different.
5. I perform better than others and they make more money.
6. I wish I had a career here but I just don't see it that way.
7. Health care premiums keep going up. Can't the company pay more?
8. We need more people to get all this work done.
9. Why can't we wear jeans Monday through Thursday instead of just Friday?
10. Can I work different hours to avoid all the traffic?

For some companies and managers, each of these issues is a dead end, and scripts are needed to get past them. For savvy organizations, though, these issues represent opportunities for improvement.

Let us look first at the even-numbered items. Smart leaders can establish ways for employees to gain more input, can provide more duties or training to overcome boredom, and can coach employees on careers or at least offer a plan for their development. These leaders can also direct their teams to suggest and implement operating efficiencies even if they cannot get additional positions. And why can't some employees work different schedules if they still get their work done?

To be sure, each of these solutions requires careful planning so the resulting activities avoid detracting from day-to-day productivity and are administered in ways that are fair to others. But remember, too, that increasing engagement and retention is hard work. Savvy managers must push themselves to see the big picture and to invest time and energy to improve engagement and retention to greatly boost productivity.

The odd-numbered items are more challenging. Sparing some employees from weekend work based on performance or length of service may be right ... or perhaps all employees should work weekends with no exceptions; each leader would need to enforce that policy. Broad-based pay questions about needing a large increase or comparing one's pay to others will likely lead to scripted responses that essentially say no. . . unless the employee performs superior to others. Regarding health care contributions, most employees know their payment amounts but not the company's and may soften their positions with scripted information about the company's cost. And maybe employees *should be permitted* to wear jeans every day ... or maybe not, depending on your company's beliefs.

Our Basic Q & A exercise reveals several striking conclusions about Stay Interviews solutions:

- Leaders who bring an open mind to the process are far more capable of identifying solutions that enhance engagement and retention. Approaching employee requests with a "Why not?" approach versus one like "That would never fly here" will lead to greater success.

- These same leaders must support company policies and executives above them by using the proper pronouns like "We" and "I" rather than separating themselves from the management team by blaming those at higher levels.

- Executives must be prepared for reasonable change; workplace and schedule flexibility is the number one policy reason for why employees leave. Executives who hear an inside voice that says "I had to drive in heavy traffic, so they should too" must adapt or they become obstacles to improvement.

- While Stay Interviews call for individualized solutions, they will also lead to healthy changes in department and company policies. Examples may include implementing flexible work schedules, permitting some work from home, or developing an effective method for instituting employee development plans.

Resources at Leaders' Fingertips

Set this book aside for a few minutes and make a list of all company resources leaders should know and have available in order for them to build the best possible stay plans. Here are a few generic resources:

- Your company's job-posting policy and process
- Developmental opportunities available in-house or via external sessions to build needed job skills
- Professional certifications for specific fields
- Mentoring, cross-training, and other ways to use in-house experts to develop colleagues
- Professional readings that expand one's base of knowledge
- Specific skills required for next-step promotions and ways to build them
- Your company's tuition reimbursement policy
- Projects that can be assigned to teach additional skills and increase one's contribution
- Ways employees can earn more money such as policies for salary increases and overtime, employee referrals, and any other award opportunities
- Your company's policies related to schedule flexibility, work from home, flextime, and related issues ... and your company's practices too, so leaders know which precedents have already been established

Nearly all of these examples require employees to take some degree of responsibility for themselves. Leaders can propose and agree to developmental plans, but employees must carry out those plans and develop their own knowledge and skills.

My own favorite developmental method from the above list is the one about assigning projects that the leader and employee agree will build valuable skills and increase one's contribution. While often times "development" is quickly associated with outside courses and certifications, the good work of Michael Lombardo and Robert Eichinger tells us that employee development results 70 percent from challenging job assignments, 20 percent from observing good work and getting feedback, and 10 percent from coursework, books, or mentors.[1] Or said another way, doing challenging work is the best way to learn, especially when coupled with immediate and clear coaching. Employees can contribute to identifying the ideal challenging work assignment too, rather than look to their manager to always identify perfect solutions.

Stay Plans for Executives

Since Stay Interviews begin at the top, let us also think through ways that stay plans may be different for executives.

Our company conducts an annual study on the issues related to executive engagement and retention in order to learn the major drivers for both. Our most recent study tells us the following about those in the C-suite who report to the CEO (see Table 5.2).

We found it interesting that "Opportunity for input" is the major driver for both staying and leaving. From the perspective of an executive who is one step below the top, this statement could mean "I want to be asked more"; "I want input into major decisions rather than hear about

Table 5.2 | Executive Survey Results	
Top 5 Reasons They Stay	**Top 5 Reasons They Would Leave**
1. Opportunity for input into company directions and decisions	1. Opportunity for input into company directions and decisions
2. Relationships with other executives and subordinates	2. Total cash compensation
3. Work/life balance	3. Future potential cash compensation
4. Work location city or state	4. Company's performance
5. Challenges in my job	5. Work/life balance

Source: 2010 Executive Retention Report: Executives Discreetly Exploring Career Options and Why the Boss Doesn't Know.

them after they have been made"; or even "I tell you what I think, and you ignore it." Regardless, the data tell us in a loud way that securing and using input is extremely important for engaging and retaining executives.

Work/life balance appears on both lists too, so it is also a principal driver for staying or leaving. Note that pay is a reason for leaving but not for staying. This finding may mean, "I wish I could make more money, but I don't think about money day to day."

Let us imagine then that your CEO has begun his or her Stay Interviews and that this is the consistent message he or she hears from direct reports: *We stay because we have input into key decisions; we enjoy working with others on our teams; we like the challenges and the life balance our job provides; and relocating to another area is unappealing at this time.*

Why would they leave based on the data above? The answers appear to be *more input, money, the company is slipping,* and *even more balance between work and home.*

The summaries in the previous two paragraphs are composites, so it is unlikely that any one person who participated in our survey provided these exact responses. But should your CEO hear this same pattern of answers, I recommend he or she rethink his or her style as it relates to seeking, listening, and truly considering the team's opinions on both big and small issues. For all of us, being consulted and heard leads to deep-seated feelings of self-worth, and we tell ourselves, "The CEO wants my opinion, so she thinks I'm smart. I really do contribute to our success here."

CEOs should also be prepared to talk about pay. Our "composite" executive is telling us he or she would likely leave for the right amount of money, and, as the saying goes, everyone has their price. My recommendation is to take the lid off all executive bonus plans and to tie bonuses to high-production goals. Then ask executives what additional resources they need, if any, to meet stretch goals by greatly improving their own and their team's productivity. The final plan will constitute the executive's own "company" with profit and loss (P&L) responsibilities. This type of plan is easier to build for executives who manage sales or production areas, and CEOs must be certain each plan is right before signing off. The message to executives becomes clear: You can make a lot of money here if you produce.

Regardless of the content of their stay plans, CEOs should conclude their stay plan discussions by asking all executives if this new plan is strong enough for them to commit to staying with the company for at least another year. CEOs should also ask each executive at least quarterly if the CEO is holding up his or her end of the deal. Our survey data make clear that many executives are looking for other jobs; more will look as the economy improves; and surprisingly, being engaged in one's work each day does not predict they will stay. So CEOs must initiate continuing discussions with critical direct reports about their work satisfaction.

One Last Thought about Solutions

The true story about the hospital food services manager in Chapter 4 underscores the value of sharing Stay Interview solutions across your company. Consider ways you can share the best results of each manager-employee stay plan so progressive ideas can transform your company. One crowdsourcing way is to provide a blog-type entry board on your company's intranet that is available only to those who manage others. This data could be sorted by topics such as development, schedule flexibility, additional pay opportunities, and other hot-button areas that are likely to surface during Stay Interview meetings.

Chapter 6 | Three-Legged Power: Integrating Stay Interviews, Exit Surveys, and Employee Surveys

In Chapter 1, I reported the shortcomings of employee surveys and exit surveys. Employee surveys were represented as good for benchmarks and bad for solutions. Exit surveys checked in as "autopsies" that rarely if ever led to positive change. Stay Interviews now become the missing link for both.

Smart companies see matching Stay Interviews and employee surveys as a hand-in-glove fit. They rely on employee surveys to benchmark employee engagement and then tailor Stay Interview questions to learn more about their engagement surveys' areas of concern. Solutions, then, become a combination of *team fixes* if many employees express an identical concern during their Stay Interviews, but there are inevitably customized solutions for individual employees as well. In short, *these companies use employee surveys for benchmark data and also to prompt Stay Interview questions. Stay Interviews then become their tools to identify the absolute best solutions for all employees or one employee.*

Exit survey data then become confirmation of employee concerns we already knew. Managers who have conducted Stay Interviews at least once per year reduce the likelihood that employees will leave by surprise and are likely to have previous insight into each employee's concern areas and to have addressed them as sufficiently like best they could.

Realistically, some employees will be less than forthcoming in both Stay Interviews and exit surveys, and some leave reasons will catch us off guard. But Stay Interviews represent a tool that equips managers to anticipate, learn, and solve employee concerns to the best of their abilities and while employees are still on board. One way to measure Stay Interviews' impact on retention is not only to count a reduced number of voluntary resignations but also to note the far fewer times that managers say of a leaving employee, "I wish I had known he felt that way." If Stay Interviews are used successfully, each manager will grow more familiar with their individual employee's innermost beliefs and concerns.

Let us address five ways to make each of these surveys more effective, beginning with exit surveys. Whether you conduct these surveys in-house or use a vendor to collect the data, these recommendations will make your data-gathering more effective as well as enable you to take real actions on the information you obtain.

Exit Survey Idea #1: Keep Surveys Short and Focused

For starters, acknowledge that the primary purpose of exit surveys is to learn why employees choose to leave, so you can spot trends in the data such as common leave reasons and leave reasons by manager, length of service, and other useful data cuts.

Ask yourself if you can discern or act on ... or if you really care about ... whether leaving employees felt good about the pay, benefits, supervisor, communications, career plans, training, or other workplace factors, if this information is not related to the reasons they left. These data often result in lengthy reports circulated around the management team with no specific recommendations. More importantly, a leaving employee may score your company low on benefits but indicate he or she is leaving because of the manager. Which piece is more pressing?

A new trend is for exit survey vendors to ask the same questions of leaving employees that they ask of continuing employees on employee surveys. Their purpose is for you to see how leaving employees feel about all aspects of their work compared to those employees who stay. Again, ask yourself if you can act on this data. Perhaps it is a way for vendors to offer an "enhanced service" that lengthens their resulting slide deck or report.

All of these survey variations result in *longer* surveys, up to 50 questions or more. Survey length likely connects to the oftentimes low participation rates of leaving employees, which by itself makes the entire exit survey process far less valid due to small sample sizes. Which survey are you more likely to complete, a 20-minute survey or a 2-minute survey ... especially when you have no vested interest in the outcome?

Exit Survey Idea #2: Report Comprehensive Leave Data

Oftentimes we have more compelling data about leaving employees than any exit survey can provide. One example is studying the length of service among leavers.

Large numbers of employees who leave early have been mis-hired or they failed to connect with their supervisors, peers, or duties. Leavers' performance data are even more revealing because losing one high performer is an exponentially larger loss than losing an average performer. Losing low performers is usually seen as a good thing, even though they represent your company's lost investment. Those who work in companies that use a 5-point performance rating scale must decide if losing a "3" employee is really a loss or if it is likely their replacement will perform their job better.

"Voluntary" and "involuntary" turnover should be reported too, as long as the organization notes that terminated employees represent a loss of investment via hiring, training, and coaching.

But probably no exit data matter more than the number and performance levels of employees who leave by manager. The Rethinking Retention Model® makes clear that managers must take responsibility for their talent, including being held accountable for retention goals. Continual patterns of high turnover for individual managers versus their peers who manage the same types of employees in the same job conditions point a long finger to those high-turnover managers as the likely cause.

HR managers often report that they circulate exit survey data and that nothing happens as a result. Those who communicate leave reasons only tell a fraction of the big retention picture. Integrating all related data not only tells the full story but leads HR managers to recommend targeted, compelling actions as a result.

Consider this question: Is it possible you have better data to understand the causes of turnover and the solutions in your HR system than you could ever get from exit surveys alone?

Exit Survey Idea #3: Ask the 'Net-Promoter' Question

Fred Reichheld of Bain & Company is the longtime guru of customer loyalty, and much of his counsel can be equally applied to employees. In a recent book, Reichheld recommends that organizations rate their customer effectiveness on just one question, that being "How likely is it that you would recommend this company to a friend or colleague?"[1] Customers, he says, should be given a response scale from 1 to 10 with 10 being the highest. Those who respond 9 or 10 become *promoters*, and those who respond from 1 to 6 become *detractors*. Reichheld refers to those who respond from 6 to 8 as *passives*. From this data, he suggests subtracting the detractors from the promoters to determine the *net-promoter* score.

Reichheld reports the very high numbers of referrals and repurchases made by promoters and the likewise high numbers of negative comments made by detractors. Based on this data, he presents a convincing argument that a company's net-promoter score is a stronger indication of success than its profits.

Exit surveys should include the net-promoter question because how leaving employees answer it is the ultimate measure of whether they think the company treated them well. Studying net-promoter patterns among managers, performance levels, and length of service will shed brighter lights on real retention issues. Of course, not all employees who choose to leave your company will give your company high scores, and this is especially true for those you *ask to leave*. But tracking net-promoter results and setting goals to improve the net-promoter score will increase your company's reputation, both inside among continuing employees and outside among potential applicants and customers.

So I recommend you add this question and weight it just as high or higher than the rest: "How likely is it that you would recommend our company as a place to work to a friend or colleague?" Then provide a scale of 1 to 10 as Reichheld recommends in order to calculate your net-promoter score for employees.

Exit Survey Idea #4: Require Managers to Conduct Exit Interviews with Supervisors

I reported in *Rethinking Retention in Good Times and Bad* that Sam Panaralla conducts exit interviews with all leaving employees and then interviews their supervisors, too.[2] Panaralla manages a consulting firm where nearly all employees produce billable hours, so losing just one employee immediately hits the bottom line. His thinking is that he not only wants to learn each employee's real reasons for leaving, but he wants each manager to learn lessons from the loss as well. In fact, Panaralla withholds signing off on new-hire requisitions until all interviews have taken place to his satisfaction.

I have recommended this technique to client companies and have seen very effective results. Supervisors now know that losing an employee leads to a "meeting with the boss," and they prepare diligently by digging to identify real reasons employees left and lessons the supervisor can learn as a result. Managers' questions may include:

- Did you hire this employee?
- Did you anticipate his or her leaving based on your Stay Interview discussions?
- What do you believe is the real reason he or she left?
- How might you have changed your ways in order to keep him or her?

- What lessons have you learned from this experience?

In most companies, supervisors either conduct the exit interview themselves, indicating the leave reason on a form, or stand by while human resources or a vendor company asks employees why they left. None of these activities drive home supervisor accountability as well as the manager-supervisor interview.

Exit Interview Idea #5: Track Improvements You Make

Few activities are more frustrating at work than those you do routinely that produce no results, yet you feel obligated to continue doing them. For most HR managers, exit interviews fit into this group.

I recommend you stop doing exit surveys ... but only if you have implemented these top four ideas completely and have seen no company improvements as a result. Measure these results by tracking data as to whether turnover falls, new hires stay longer, managers with high turnover reduce their turnover, net-promoter scores improve, or high performers stay longer. Measure these results also by anecdote, asking and listening to managers about lessons they have learned and about whether they hire and coach more carefully.

Validate, too, whether fewer leave reasons catch you and your managers by surprise. Implementing Stay Interviews and improving exit surveys is a strong combination for not only improving retention and engagement but also for ramping up the likelihood that those who leave could not have been retained.

To summarize the exit survey recommendations:

- Be quick.
- Be thorough.

- Be leading edge.
- Be collaborative.
- And be prudent by making exit surveys improve your organization, or stop doing them.

Now let us move on to five ideas to improve employee surveys.

Employee Survey Idea #1: Keep These Surveys Short Too and Frequent

Use employee surveys for (1) benchmarks to measure progress by organization, units, and managers and (2) to sniff out employee concerns about major workplace issues. For example, ask for opinions about communications in one question rather than in five more specific questions. If employees indicate communications are a concern, structure a Stay Interview question so supervisors can probe more deeply. Then while supervisors build local solutions that are based on their team's input, human resources can look over company-wide Stay Interview data to identify trends that lead to company-wide solutions as well.

Asking fewer questions opens the door to asking questions more often. Company intranets make asking employees to respond to 10 or so questions easy when they log in each day, so data is acquired with little fuss. Gone should be the days when employees are sequestered into a room and told they have 45 minutes to complete the company survey and then "all pencils down!"

Managers will welcome more frequent surveys too, as opposed to being stuck on a substandard score for a year or more. They also will perform better as coaches, knowing that their teams will rate them more frequently.

Employee Survey Idea #2: Schedule Employee Surveys to Precede Stay Interviews

Map out a 3-year plan for conducting performance reviews, employee surveys, and Stay Interviews. Separate performance reviews and Stay Interviews so employees see a clear difference between perceptions of their performance and ways the company can engage and retain them. Plan, too, for Stay Interviews to follow within a month or so of employee survey results so Stay Interview questions can be customized to address areas of concern expressed on the survey.

The primary variable here is whether your company conducts performance reviews at the same time for all or most employees or conducts them on each employee's anniversary month. If employees are reviewed simultaneously, schedule Stay Interviews at the same time, about six months after performance reviews. Then Stay Interviews can be conducted one month after survey results are available. If performance reviews are conducted on employees' anniversary month, conduct their Stay Interviews six months after their performance reviews, and use the most recent employee survey data available to construct the Stay Interview questions.

Employee Survey Idea #3: Ask the "Net-Promoter" Question Here, Too

The net-promoter question provides a similar benefit in employee surveys as it does in exit surveys. Your executives will want to know whether your organization's score is increasing or decreasing as well as know the same for each of your managers. Survey designers usually recommend including one or a small number of questions that are more important than others so that together they form the ultimate score for employee satisfaction or engagement. Use the net-promoter calculation as either that ultimate metric or one of a few questions that compose it.

Employee Survey Idea #4: Appoint Yourself Quality Manager for All Survey Action Plans

Managers know the employee survey drill ... get results, compare benchmark scores, and submit a report with improvement actions. While some of these action items are creative and effective, others "check the box" by committing to nonspecific recognition events and other usual suspects that substitute for real leadership. The real leadership-improvement opportunity in these circumstances is yours.

Commit yourself to challenge these managers by probing for details regarding why, how, and when. This task can initially be done by revising the employee survey action form so action plans are more than paragraphs, but some managers require in-person or remote discussions that present hard questions to ultimately derive an improvement plan that really makes a difference. Ideally, the executive who oversees that manager should participate and lead such a meeting, but when you are the best one suited to help, volunteer with strength to help.

Take the identical approach with Stay Interview improvement plans, too. Employee development plans offer a prime example as these can range from highly specific to nearly undefined. Ask yourself if the proposed activities and completion dates would really make that employee both a better performer and more inclined to engage and stay. If the answer is no, suggest specific improvements. The real leadership-improvement opportunity in these circumstances is yours.

Employee Survey Idea #5: Hold Managers Accountable for Achieving a Survey Standard

Leaders on all levels are accountable for profits, customer service, quality, staying within budgets, and other standard performance metrics, and I have recommended in this book that they also be held accountable for employee retention. Most organizations track how their managers scored on employee surveys, but few CEOs treat that score as an equal to profits, service, and the rest.

So think through how your executives handle managers whose teams treat customers poorly (for example, their customer service scores are weak). Are these scores circulated on a one-time report with the assumption that low-scoring managers will take appropriate actions? Or do executives meet with these managers to develop an improvement plan that the manager must ultimately achieve or suffer from lower bonus payments or even termination?

Cliches like "inspect what you expect" apply here. Psychology 101 taught us that humans and even nonhumans respond to stimuli. If necessary, ask your executive team members whether they see managers' employee survey scores as equal to other key metrics, and then summarize for them the usual follow-up activities and potential consequences. The ultimate question will be, "If you don't act on this data in ways that make it useful, why do we do the survey at all?"

To summarize employee survey recommendations:

- Be quick, be frequent.
- Be timely to integrate with Stay Interviews.
- Be leading edge here, too.
- Be a quality control leader.

- Be effective by influencing executives to hold managers accountable … and if necessary be courageous about doing so

Why Not Initiate a People-Management Balanced Scorecard?

Dashboards, scorecards, and other new-look reporting mechanisms are trendy and very useful for reporting operational metrics, so why not develop one for people management too? You now have at your fingertips for each manager:

- Employee survey scores versus the company score and a standard
- Employee turnover versus the company percent and a standard
- Employee turnover by reasons for leaving
- Employee turnover by performance
- Employee turnover by length of service
- Net-promoter scores of current and exiting employees

You can also add to this data all managers' revenue per employee to see if they use their assigned positions effectively. And data related to net profits, quality, and customer service are direct reflections of how well managers lead their team compared with how well peer managers lead.

CEOs are accustomed to reviewing sales, service, and other operational metrics daily, often by 6 a.m. People-management data are not only less available for them but also more diffused. Rarely are these data incorporated into one clear and concise report. And any report that presents data must also present them by individual managers by name in order to cause substantial change.

People-management data on all levels predict the future, whereas daily operational data talk only about today. Those HR managers who want to demonstrate each managers' responsibility to effectively manage their teams must do so with data because most CEOs and CFOs are "numbers people" first. Influence sometimes requires translation. The Rethinking Retention Model® presents another example of translation; the very best way to influence CEOs to hold managers accountable for turnover is to ask Finance to place a cost on turnover first.

So make a list of your tasks for today, this month, and this year, and circle the ones that are truly strategic, that will drive your company forward in the eyes of your CEO. Then consider the forever value of providing him or her with comprehensive people-management data by organization, departments, and managers, each month or more frequently. Your tasks will be achieved far more easily if your executives and managers are locking onto the data your are making available to them.

Chapter 7 | The Stay Interview Game

Following are seven scenarios representing different managers' approaches for leading their Stay Interviews. Each scenario offers a complex challenge, and your role is to identify the strengths and weaknesses of each manager's approach. Later we will ask you to rank-order each manager's effectiveness from most to least effective and then ask you to compare your answers to ours.

Please note that some of these examples represent extremes. Most Stay Interviews conducted by your company will be smoother and more congenial. But there may be a few that offer challenges that must be addressed, and the Stay Interview Game will prepare you and your managers for those challenges.

Scenario #1: We Call During Dinner

John's title at WCDD call center is team leader. The company's name is based on the initials of its four founding partners, but employees refer to the company as "We call during dinner."

John's duties are to manage a team of 15 agents who have various levels of experience and skills. Because John has so many direct reports, most of his day is spent listening to calls and helping his agents solve problems. And oftentimes he is on the phones himself because of high turnover.

Two times each month John sits with each agent individually to conduct quality control meetings where together they listen to one of that agent's recorded calls which John has graded against the protocols the agent learned in training. The grading scale is from a low of 60 to a high of 100. Agents have learned that earning a score of 100 is nearly impossible, like Olympic scoring in that something is surely less than perfect.

Conducting Stay Interviews made John uneasy. He learned supervision from watching those above him, so his style is "Is everything OK?" and "Here's what you can do better." Turnover is 80 percent at John's center, and his own agents stay about as long, or short, as the rest. When one quits, John knows it is because the job is boring, the pay is low, and "that's the way young people are" ... even though John is only 26.

John attended Stay Interview training and then told his team members what he was instructed to say, that he wanted to meet with them one-on-one to learn why they stay as well as how he could help them become more engaged and stay longer. Having never heard these types of words from John before, his team froze in surprise.

John's initial reluctance now turned to escape. He sought out Wendy, his manager, to explain that he was too busy to hold one more individual meeting with each agent that month so he planned to merge the Stay Interview discussion into one of the monitoring meetings. John knew this method would increase his own confidence and give him control of the discussion since he would begin the meeting telling the agent how many points she scored below 100 on the call they would listen to together. But Wendy explained that they all heard in training that the Stay Interview had to be held as a separate meeting, independent of any performance discussion. For John, playing the "busy card" did not work.

John scheduled his first Stay Interview meeting with Maria, a 4-year veteran with WCDD. John and Maria had always gotten along well, so John thought he would start with someone who would make his first meeting easy.

John began the meeting by asking Maria what she liked about her work, and Maria's answer was vanilla ... "job is OK; people are OK; customers get rude sometimes; commute is long when school is in session." John then asked Maria what she did not like, and Maria paused first and then said the following. "John, we all know you are having these meetings because you have to. You seem like an OK guy but none of us feel like you really care about us. We've all talked about this since you mentioned these meetings last week, and we just don't think telling you our problems is going to do any good."

John's mind flashed to Wendy first, knowing that she put him in this position because she would not let him combine this meeting with the monitoring session. But he knew he had to say something back.

"Well ... ," he began, "of course I care about you. It's just that it's so hard to show that when my job is to tell you what you can do better." John heard himself say those words and knew it was a cop-out but still hoped Maria would buy it.

She did not buy it. Maria entered the meeting knowing her years of experience made her the informal spokesperson for the team. Over the next 20 minutes, she told John that while having more "things" at work would be nice ... "better schedules, more socials, maybe even vision care" ... she observed that the team just wanted to feel better during their 40 hours at work and that changes in his behavior could be the answer.

"So you're blaming me for all of the problems in WCDD, huh?" John fired back. And he was just warming up. John went on to say that he could not control the pay scale, that he knew agents were expected to cram too much into calls, and that his manager and his job did not permit him time to be nice to each agent on his team. Then John drove home two points out of sheer frustration. "Besides, I had to work under these conditions when I started, so you have to work under them, too. And when did the team ever do anything nice for me?"

Maria knew she was in too deep to bail so she made a brave suggestion. "John," she said in a softer tone, "I think we should step back a little and think about all that's been said here. How about if we meet again tomorrow morning and talk about ways we can make this better, for all of us? I promise I will keep all that we've said to myself between now and then."

John mumbled his OK, not realizing that he had just lost control of his Stay Interview meeting.

That night John's mind raced back to all that he said and should have said. The emotional side told him what our minds tell us when we hear bad news at work about others' negative feelings for us ... that our long hours are not appreciated and that we do not make enough money to take this ... so we should flee.

Near morning, though, John knew Maria was at least a little right and that he could try harder, be nicer, reach out more, be more positive, and look for reasons to actually like the members of his team. Or at least most of them.

While John was flopping from anger to acceptance, Maria knew she had volunteered for a job with deep consequences. She could emerge as a hero to John *and* the team, or she might face "angry John" again in the morning and have hurt her relationship with him forever. And he *is* the boss.

At 9 a.m., Maria strode into John's work area and suggested they find a quiet corner in the break room and have a cup of coffee. John followed and still did not know just what he would say. Once they settled into their table, Maria said the following: "John, I thought a lot about this last night, and I believe that you not only *can* become a caring supervisor but that you *want* to be one."

From there the conversation went easy. Maria's opening line made John know that *she liked him and cared about him.* John felt more human now and less of a work machine. Together, he and Maria worked out a plan of ideas whereby John would make himself more available to the team, begin each monitoring session with at least three compliments, go out of his way to learn a few personal things about each agent so he could ask about them, and focus on smiling more and frowning less. The only hard part for John was realizing that his changed behaviors would be an indicator that he had been "wrong" before, but over time he decided that was OK.

Toward the end of the meeting, John told Maria he would hold a team meeting to announce "the new John." Not good, Maria said. Start the new ways immediately, but let each agent have his or her say in the ensuing Stay Interviews so all will have contributed to the solutions. "Besides," she said, "you really don't know what else you'll hear because we all see things a little differently."

Two months later, John was a better supervisor because the Stay Interview feedback guided him to new behaviors. He was a combination of "new John" mixed with some of "old John," inconsistent for sure, but better. And engagement and retention improved across his team as a result.

John's Stay Interview Strengths	John's Stay Interview Shortcomings

Scenario #2: Tipping Cows

Brenda's eyes glanced toward the floor when she heard her manager say she wanted to meet with team members to learn why they stay. Brenda was unhappy and was embarrassed about her problems but faked being OK day to day.

Raised and living in a rural Midwestern town, Brenda caught the nursing bug early and was fortunate her parents could help her through college. After graduation, a friend-of-the-family doctor was setting up shop and asked Brenda to join. She did and helped that doctor treat her community's patients for 23 years. Brenda's skills were a perfect match for providing individualized, caring treatment for those who needed it.

Out of the blue, the doctor announced his early retirement. He told Brenda that the office lease would expire soon, that he had found a buyer for his equipment, and that he was confident his patients could find new sources of care. He also knew the local community hospital was expanding and certainly Brenda could find work there.

Still dazed, Brenda proceeded to apply at the hospital. She learned there were immediate openings and believed treating patients was the same regardless of the setting. Her commute was a few miles longer since she had to drive into town but that was OK. She had also been told that she would have to learn technology skills that were new to her, as the hospital had recently installed a new system for nurses to record and track their patients' treatments and medications.

Brenda's first week included detailed and extensive training on computers and technology. Each nurse was anchored to a laptop on a wheeled cart that they pushed from room to room. Other nurses referred to these carts as COWs for "computers on wheels." The chuckle expression when navigating tight spaces was to say, "Don't tip your COW!"

Brenda's face fell when hearing the Stay Interview announcement because she struggled with technology and everyone in the room knew it ... except her manager, Billie. Brenda's technology experience at the doctor's office was thin because the doctor had never invested in anything beyond Microsoft Office. Worse for Brenda, she had asked for help from so many of her peers that they were losing patience with her. It was not that Brenda was afraid to ask for help. Instead, she really believed she could never learn to use the software because technology frightened her. She feared she was too old to learn.

On "Stay Interview day," Brenda confessed. Billie had heard snippets from other nurses about Brenda's computer shortcomings and felt good that the issue was now on the table. Billie saw Brenda's need as easy to pinpoint, that she required more classroom training and a peer coach who would be open to Brenda's questions. Brenda nodded that this would help yet felt deep inside that no amount of training could help her conquer her fear. It was like a chronic illness that would never go away.

During the meeting, Brenda also surfaced a second concern about schedules. During her interviews, Brenda heard clearly that her hospital job would require working a fair share of weekends and holidays. This schedule was far removed from the doctor's office where the hours were weekdays and daylight and all after-hour emergencies were referred to 9-1-1 or to the hospital. In fact, Brenda had not worked a Friday afternoon in her life.

Brenda explained the usual reasons why weekend and holiday work was unattractive ... family events, church, errands, overnight guests ... but knew her peers had the same obstacles to overcome. So she proposed an advantage she could offer Billie in order to gain a schedule preference in order that she could at least pick which holidays she worked rather than have them be selected by chance.

The advantage Brenda offered was that she would agree to be the first nurse called when a night-shift nurse called in sick, as long as she was not required to work three consecutive shifts. Brenda saw this plan as a win-win, that Billie would know she had a guaranteed fill-in without straining her relationships by calling others on the team. Brenda was willing to tolerate these life interruptions to earn choices regarding holidays but she also craved the overtime she would earn as a result.

Unfortunately for Brenda, her "advantage plan" fell flat. Billie listened carefully but knew early on that she could not agree to Brenda's idea without giving all others on the team the same opportunity. Billie also knew that the scheduling plan in place was ultimately fair and that it treated everyone in an identical way, and that is the way she wanted it.

Billie explained her reasons for rejecting Brenda's idea in a clear, firm, and professional way. She smiled as she told Brenda how moving from the schedule-friendly world of the doctor's office must be hard and that she privately questioned whether Brenda could make that adjustment before hiring her. She concluded by saying that others on the team may want the same arrangement Brenda has proposed and that she was unwilling to stir the schedule pot by advancing it.

Billie then asked Brenda if she had any other things to discuss. Brenda said no, that she was looking forward to finally grasping the technology that she had so far been unable to learn. When she got home that night, Brenda understood that the feared technology was not going away, and neither was weekend and holiday work.

One month later, Billie saw Brenda in the hall. Walking together, Brenda told Billie that the computer training had helped but that the peer mentor idea gave her the biggest boost of confidence which was what she really needed. Billie congratulated Brenda on advancing her skills and then went about her way.

Billie's Stay Interview Strengths	Billie's Stay Interview Shortcomings
_____	_____
_____	_____
_____	_____
_____	_____
_____	_____
_____	_____
_____	_____

Scenario #3: RENRON Consulting

Two years ago, Charles took his recently earned MBA to RENRON Consulting Company, choosing RENRON over several others that made very attractive offers. Charles chose RENRON for several reasons, not the least of which was that RENRON was perceived globally as one of the top three firms of its type.

But the last year had not been kind to RENRON. A series of ethics violations and resulting lawsuits had weakened both its stock value and its international reputation. There were days when Charles regretted his choice of employers.

On "Stay Interview day," both Charles and his manager, Eleanor, knew this topic would dominate their discussion. Eleanor took the lead and began the meeting by asking Charles his most recent thoughts on the topic. Charles replied, "I have no new thoughts, Eleanor, just the same ones. How did our executives put us in this position, and what are they going to do about it?"

Eleanor had prepared diligently and read from her notes: on this date the company reiterated its statement of ethics; on another date the board appointed a special committee to review the policies that had caused the problems; and on another date the company announced all executives, managers, and consultants would take a newly designed ethics course and sign off that they would act in ethical ways on behalf of the company.

These were old words to Charles. He knew he was far too distant from the source of the fixes to feel comfortable with his future. And headhunters were calling every week.

Feeling Charles' frustration, Eleanor said the following: "I know you are frustrated, Charles, and I am too. But I'm telling you all that I know. What else can I do to help you believe RENRON is pulling itself out of the problem and will soon be on the road to full recovery? How can I assure you that we will soon be back in the top three?"

The part Charles heard was "I'm telling you all that I know." He realized that Eleanor's word was "too small" for him, that he needed to be assured by a higher source, especially one who could tell him about the problems and solutions in more detail. Subconsciously, what Charles really needed was to feel "on the inside" of the closed-door discussions, a status no one on his level had been privy to.

"I just need to hear it from someone higher," was the sentence Charles chose to express his position.

Smart Eleanor was reading the situation accurately and realized a time-out was in order. "Let me think about your concern, Charles. Can we meet again on Thursday?"

That afternoon, Eleanor asked Mitchell, her manager, if they could talk for few minutes. Eleanor suggested to Mitchell that together they identify someone for Charles to meet with whom Charles would see as an insider yet also as a person who would effectively assure Charles that everything would be OK. Mitchell pushed back, expressing a legitimate concern that Charles should receive no special treatment. Knowing Mitchell as she did, Eleanor expected this objection. After much discussion, she sold Mitchell on the idea that since she scheduled a monthly lunch meeting with each member of her team, it would be OK to invite an executive to join her lunch with Charles the following month.

The discussion then turned to which executive to choose, and Mitchell volunteered himself. Eleanor anticipated this stage in their meeting too, as Mitchell saw himself as a highly respected executive who was mentor to all. But Eleanor also knew that she needed a new face, someone who Charles knew by very strong reputation and whom he would see as flattering to meet. Thinking further, Eleanor knew she needed to secure a lunch date with someone whose very presence Charles would see as testimony to his own growing stature at RENRON.

Eleanor knew how to manage Mitchell. She proceeded to tell him all the reasons he would be a great choice and concluded by saying that she needed a new face. He reluctantly agreed, and together they decided the best choice was Mercedes, who was the divisional executive for the national consulting group. Eleanor had worked closely over the years with Mercedes, and Mitchell agreed she should contact Mercedes on her own.

From this point forward, Eleanor put the finishing touches on her plan. She first briefed Mercedes on Charles' concern and secured her agreement for lunch. She then asked Charles if inviting Mercedes to join their monthly lunch meeting would give him the right opportunity to discuss his thoughts with an executive. Charles beamed and left her office with his head held high.

Privately, Eleanor knew that she was giving Charles privileged treatment over his peers and could think of no way to disguise it. Ultimately she decided that Charles was one of her best performers who had the greatest potential, so all means should be used to keep him and to engage him. Over time she might ask Mercedes to join her for other team member lunches, so she convinced herself that Mercedes' lunch with Charles was the first of many.

Two weeks later, Mercedes joined Charles and Eleanor for lunch. After exchanging pleasantries and ordering their meals, Eleanor opened the discussion by inviting Charles to state his concerns. After hearing them, Mercedes gave essentially the same response Eleanor had given Charles weeks before. She added a detail here and there that Charles had not heard, but more importantly she positioned the recent goings-on within the context of RENRON's solid history of industry leadership and ethical behavior.

After lunch, Eleanor accompanied Charles to his office and asked for his impressions. Glowing in the aftermath of a private executive briefing, Charles said he was proud to be a member of RENRON. Eleanor knew she had patched Charles' emotional need, even though he believed what he needed was more information.

Eleanor's Stay Interview Strengths	Eleanor's Stay Interview Shortcomings
_____	_____
_____	_____
_____	_____
_____	_____
_____	_____
_____	_____
_____	_____

Scenario #4: Parts-Is-Parts

Robert had now completed seven Stay Interviews and had his routine down. As GM of Parts-Is-Parts Fried Chicken store #66, Robert knew the easy part about satisfying his employees was that their jobs were not complicated. So far he had fixed a few relationships among peers, learned a thing or two about his own style, and explained to one team member why the company could not pay more for her family's health insurance. With seven meetings done, Robert felt like a real problem-solver.

Robert had also completed the Stay Interviews for the most valued members of his team and was now moving into the group he considered to be "phase two." These were the passive, steady employees who had been there forever. Next up was James, a 9-year veteran who loved to fry chicken. James had a ready smile for everyone that came straight from his heart, although it came via the exposure of a missing front tooth.

Robert began with his usual introduction, exclaiming how he wanted to build his Parts-Is-Parts store into the very best one where all team members wanted to come to work. He then asked James how he could make his job better.

James threw a curve. Smiling as always, he told Robert that he had given his all for nine full years and that it was time he got his due. James wanted to be promoted to shift leader and then within two years land a coveted spot in the Parts-Is-Parts management training program.

Stunned, Robert searched for an easy sentence that would reduce James' expectations. After an uncomfortable few seconds he settled on this one: "Why, James, would you ever want the headaches that come with managing people?"

Robert knew he had to nip this wish in the bud and resorted to telling James all of the reasons why moving up the ladder would make him unhappy. But within a minute Robert could hear himself babbling and knew he had been caught off guard. He then said the magic phrase every smart manager says during Stay Interviews that take on sudden twists: "Why don't you give me a few days to think about this, James, and let's talk again on Friday."

Robert was in a pickle he had to solve on his own. Sponsoring James upstream to the next level would lead to you-gotta-be-kidding glances and worse. Even if he found a way to promote James to shift leader, the Parts-Is-Parts management training program offered such stiff competition that James had no chance of getting in. In a way this put even more pressure on Robert because he could blame the company for James' not winning a spot in the training program, but he had no defense for not promoting James to shift leader. That decision was his and his alone.

Robert's decision became clear ... when in doubt, stall. He wrote out six questions to ask James about why he wanted to become shift leader without ever mentioning the management training program. A few of the questions were hypothetical that used current employees as examples, such as how would you handle Alicia if she came in late two days in a row. Instead of just asking for answers, Robert asked James to act out his responses, believing James might stumble by having to say out loud the exact words he would use to solve a common employee issue.

But James' answers were pretty good. In fact, Robert realized that James was unintentionally instructing him on how to handle people-management situations by presenting approaches and solutions Robert had never considered on his own. Somehow, beneath the cloak of this grease-stained apron was the mind of a potential people-leader.

Flummoxed again, Robert bought more time. "Let's meet again next week," he said. James beamed back approvingly through the gap in his teeth.

For Robert, the decision-making flowchart had become clear. Even if James had hidden talents, no one would believe it. So if he wanted to give James a legitimate opportunity to become shift leader, he had to find a way for others to see the undiscovered side of James. Robert also knew there was Plan B, which was to give James a "nonlegitimate opportunity," in other words to fake that he would help with no intentions of ever truly sponsoring him.

Robert eventually decided on Plan A, or at least a hybrid version. Since shift leader positions became available every six months or so, he had time to build his plan. Step one, he decided, was to elevate James to a minor leadership role within the store in order for James to demonstrate his newly disclosed abilities. Robert sensed that he could never promote James without finding a way to sell him in advance to his peers.

During their next meeting, Robert opened by saying the following to James: "Last week you told me some really good ideas about how you would approach team members, James, and I was pretty impressed. I have an idea for you that is a good next step, and I want to hear your opinion about it. But before I tell it to you, I want you to know that I can never promise you a promotion to shift leader or especially to the Parts-Is-Parts management training program because there are many employees in addition to you who want those jobs. But by working together, hopefully we can put you in a position to compete. How does this sound so far?"

James nodded and leaned forward. The idea, Robert explained, was for James to take on a training role in the weekly team meetings. Each week James would identify a piece of one job and provide a tip and then ask the team to contribute additional tips. For example, week one's tip would be things to tell yourself so that you would keep smiling when a customer becomes rude. After each meeting James would summarize the ideas and post them on the bulletin board by the time clock. James would preview his comments in advance with Robert each week, and they could anticipate other good ideas they would hear from the team.

Robert knew the risks involved. A few members of his team would for sure question why James got such a plum role that made him look superior to them. This situation would lead to inevitable gossip and nonproductive chatter among the team. Additionally, Robert sometimes invited his manager to these meetings, and he expected to be questioned about his judgment.

But after much thought, Robert saw James as an employee worth investing in. His bet was that after two meetings all doubts would be dismissed and that his team and manager would see the wisdom of his decision. And once sold, he then had a legitimate choice to move James into the next shift leader position or to recommend him for the same position in another store.

Robert's best skill in responding to James was probably buying time, and he had done it again. And when the next shift leader position came open, Robert would have much more information on James to make an insightful decision.

Robert's Stay Interview Strengths	Robert's Stay Interview Shortcomings

Scenario #5: Burning Bridges

Paul knew he was last on the Stay Interview schedule. Being 52, he wondered if the meeting sequence was based on age. One month ago Shirley, his manager, announced the Stay Interview process and said she would reach out to each team member individually. Since then Paul watched each of his younger peers go in and out of Shirley's office and then heard scuttlebutt regarding the promises she had made ... usually more training that could lead to more money and promotions.

Paul did not mind being last, he told himself, because *he* might meet with himself last, too. Paul was a lifer, having joined New-Age Engineering right out of college, and never made a ripple about leaving or wanting something more. "Team player" was Paul's mantra, day to day, decade to decade.

But Paul knew too that the recession has sapped his 401(k) and that he needed to make more money to retire in 10 years. So the timing of his Stay Interview was not nearly as important as the outcome. And he was confident he would leave with a good plan as the other employees had, since his performance appraisals had always been outstanding.

When the big day came, Paul received a text from Shirley's assistant asking if he could move the meeting to the following Tuesday. As was his way, Paul tapped back with a smiley face and said that would be fine. Come Tuesday, Paul arrived at Shirley's office early with prepared notes in hand. Though Shirley arrived late, Paul maintained his optimism.

Shirley began the meeting with a warm greeting and then thanked Paul for his years of outstanding service. She then said she was pleased that Paul was on a steady course, and his contributions were just as she needed them to be.

Paul was waiting for questions that would cue his notes, but as he listened to Shirley he feared they would never come. Finally he interrupted and said, "Shirley, I need more money, and I know I can contribute more."

At just that moment, Shirley's Blackberry buzzed, and she checked the message. Through a thin smile she asked Paul's forgiveness and sent a lengthy response.

Paul knew he had to lead the discussion and proceeded with uncharacteristic bravado. For most of his career, he said, he had been pigeonholed into designing bridges and similar structures. This work left him with fewer projects than young engineers who had learned in college to use various software products to do different types of work. Paul went on to say that his strongest computer-design skill was the result of a company-sponsored course. Virtually all of his college training was obsolete.

Paul knew he needed more training in order to be more valuable. His deepest fear was that the economy would hit another downturn and that he could be laid off. And in Paul's mind, being laid off and "getting a package" brought the same dead-end result. He could not take a lump sum in place of 10 more years of work and provide for his family as he intended. And without more training he was probably not employable by another firm.

Paul explained his predicament in lucid terms to Shirley. From his perspective, the problem had a simple solution, which he was leading up to. Shirley's perspective, however, was that this meeting should already be over. Paul was "parked" in her mind and rightfully restricted to bridge design and similar projects. Her younger team members were better trained, more versatile, and cheaper to pay. Paul should be glad to coast to retirement and should hope she retained him that long.

Not knowing Shirley's thoughts, Paul proceeded to lay out his plan. On his own he had discovered four university courses he could take by correspondence that would supplement his knowledge and therefore his contribution. Paul knew that by completing these courses and doing complementary work assignments, he would ensure his place in the workforce for 10 years or more, whether employed by New-Age or another firm. The total cost for Paul's plan was less than $20,000, and he asked Shirley to support him.

Shirley's answer was no but she held off on saying it. Instead she told Paul she had planned just 20 minutes for this meeting, and their time was up. "You've laid a lot on me, Paul. Let me get back to you with my answer. I'll need to check this with those above me." Paul nodded, smiled, and extended his hand in partnership before he left Shirley's office.

During the next few days Paul's proposal did not make Shirley's top 10. She had many distractions about current work getting done, as even the young smart ones could get off track. But seeing Paul in the hallways and cafeteria reminded her that she had to tell him the bad news. This decision was easy for Shirley. It made no sense to invest money in Paul when she could invest it instead in someone with more potential and especially with more years to contribute. "Besides," she told herself, "no one here really listens to Paul, so his being disappointed won't resonate with the rest of the team. He's a loner who has served his time and gotten just what he deserved. As long as I can keep him employed," she reasoned, "I have been a fair manager even if he never agrees." Shirley also knew she did not need any help from her own manager to make this decision. Her thinking and conscience were equally clear.

Nine days later, Shirley invited Paul in for a "5-minute chat." She told Paul that she was pleased with his current contributions and saw no reason to trouble him to take additional courses. She promised to seek extra projects for him when circumstances permitted and again thanked him for all he had contributed to New-Age Engineering.

Shirley's Stay Interview Strengths	Shirley's Stay Interview Shortcomings

Scenario #6: Rump Roast

"Thank you for shopping with us, ma'am," Lester said for the 37th time that day. Today was Saturday at Shamrock Supermarket, the week's busiest day. For Lester, Saturdays just offered more of the same boring work.

Lester joined the company to bag groceries while still in high school. After graduation he stayed on and talked his way into the butcher shop, where he learned the fundamentals of carving and packaging. On Saturdays he spends much of his time in the back room preparing custom orders. But Lester has found that after two years of butchering, every day seems like another serving of rump roast.

Lester told the same to his manager, Kelly, during his Stay Interview. Kelly knew this grievance would surface but also knew there were no easy answers. Many employees stood ahead of Lester for consideration for other positions. Besides, two years did not seem like a long enough time for Lester to complain his way to another position.

Kelly's dilemma was compounded by Lester's behavior. He came to work each day and completed more work than most. He was reliable, volunteered to help others, and was good with customers when he got the chance. The flip side was that Lester could not manage his mouth as he constantly chattered toward anyone in reach about his life and his opinions of Shamrock.

Lester's daily menu of information included comments about his nagging wife, his unappreciative children, and his neighbor who will not cut his grass, as well as running commentaries on politics, religion, and the economy. Lester of course believed his positions were always right, and somewhere down deep he had adopted the idea that he was also entertaining. His peers would call him anything but and referred to him behind his back with names that were similar to rump roast.

Kelly knew this situation was out of control but had done nothing to stop it. Early on she thought Lester would "outgrow it," that running at the mouth was his way of adjusting to a new circumstance. Then once or twice she sent him a discouraging glance and hoped he would take the hint. But hints could not stop this man who was on a subconscious, ego-driven mission to lead others toward his every conviction.

Until now, Lester had gotten by because Kelly basically ignored him. Other members of the team had little faith that Kelly would ever confront him, so they complained among themselves but said nothing to her. Kelly's position morphed into appreciating Lester's productivity and tolerating his shortcomings. Besides, she thought, nobody seemed too concerned about Lester's babbles.

But now he wanted a promotion or at least a transfer to another area. Kelly grimaced to herself because her one supervisory class had taught her that she needed to be strong.

As the Stay Interview continued, Kelly absorbed Lester's complaints about the redundancy of his work. Lester spoke with full-force confidence that Kelly would move him because he had only heard good things about his work. And he knew he was always right.

Kelly allowed Lester to delve into great detail about his frustrations in order to procrastinate her role in the meeting because she did not know how to approach him. When he finally stopped talking, she said this: "Lester, we have a problem we need to discuss, and you are going to have to overcome this problem before I consider you for another position."

Kelly found her spine and told Lester all that she knew and felt about his expressing his opinions. Lester responded by talking, of course, and initially defended that his opinions were right. Kelly redirected the exchange to present Lester's ramblings as distracting from work, regardless of their accuracy. This concept was hard for Lester to grasp because above all else he saw himself as an entertainer, someone who made everyone's day at work better.

After 45 minutes of verbal jousting, Lester asked Kelly why she had not told him this before. Partly to shift the blame, he told Kelly he had come into his Stay Interview to move his career forward with Shamrock but now felt he was taking a step back. Kelly felt a brief urge to say something apologetic but instead said, "I know this is not what you came to hear, Lester, but you need to hear it."

Lester took on Kelly's feedback like the five stages of death. In the denial stage, he asked a few peers if his opinions really bothered them and learned indeed they did. These talks were difficult for both sides because not only did they require candor, but Lester still defended his opinions as correct.

Ultimately, Lester toned down his rhetoric and continued to do a good job. Kelly monitored his ramblings and improved a bit at delivering timely feedback. She also looked for positive things to say. For Lester, work became less fun because he had to place his mouth on guard, and he wondered if others really liked him since they had held back before. This meant they had not been straight, he told himself, including Kelly. So while he stayed in the butcher shop, he wondered if Shamrock was still the right place for him to work.

Kelly's Stay Interview Strengths	Kelly's Stay Interview Shortcomings

Scenario #7: Happy Endings

The employee survey results were in, and Marvin wasn't happy.

Marvin is the executive director of Happy Endings Nursing Home, one of many owned by Sunshine Corporation. Sunshine followed the demographic paths of retirees to build hundreds of nursing homes across the southern part of the U.S. with heavy clusters in Florida, Texas, and Arizona.

This pathway led to a shortage of nursing home employees during any economy. Because facilities are built where retirees relocate, they tend to be clustered in narrow geographic areas. Facilities then compete for local talent, but much of that talent prefers to work anywhere else. Nursing home employees must have big hearts, strong wills, and high tolerance for sights, sounds, and smells that others would abandon.

Marvin was keenly aware that employee retention and engagement drove his service levels up ... or down. Whereas the Sunshine headquarters team accepted high turnover as inevitable for the industry, Marvin monitored his carefully. During the past three years he had lost an average of 70 percent of his team each year.

Marvin's engagement survey results looked about the same as last year's. The overall engagement index was down two points. And like last year, the main employee concerns appeared to be pay, schedules, careers, and communication.

Marvin was perplexed. He could not understand how last year's solutions had not yielded better results. Sure, pay would always be an issue, and Marvin privately questioned whether any employees would reveal in a survey that they actually liked their pay. He certainly would not.

Marvin tried to make schedules better but found the smarter fix was to hire employees who wanted the unpopular schedules, at least he thought. For careers, Marvin brought in a local consultant to present a three-part course teaching employees to take charge of their own careers, and he promised his team that all openings would be posted immediately. Communication, he figured, was the easiest of all to fix because he needed to do a better job staying in touch with the team. So Marvin implemented town hall meetings each quarter. He even came in at 5 a.m. to meet with the night shift.

Why, then, had survey scores not gone up? And what could he do differently this year?

Enter a new idea. Always checking on new people-management trends, Marvin had heard about Stay Interviews as an alternative to surveys. What might happen, he wondered, if he designed Stay Interview questions that aligned with the weakest areas of his survey results and as a result learned the fixes employees really wanted instead of the best ones he could invent?

Marvin explained this idea to his management team, and they responded so-so at best. But Marvin knew his idea was a winner and would not back off. He returned to his office and wrote out one question each about pay, schedules, careers, and communication. The next day he told his management team his plan, that he would meet with each of them to ask the four questions and that they would then in turn ask their direct reports, down to the first-line employees. From there, he told them, together they would create real solutions that worked versus ones like he implemented last year.

Marvin's team went easy on him during their Stay Interviews. They were actually a pretty pleased bunch, but they also knew Stay Interviews were Marvin's pet project, and they wanted him to feel good about their meetings. The management group's interviews with their teams, though, produced real frustration. While a few wanted pay increases or career help, most wanted things that only their immediate supervisor could provide. As the Stay Interviews proceeded down the organization, a trend became clear: most employees desired changes that only a better supervisor could provide, not a company-wide program.

Marvin had told his management team that one month out they would meet to review all Stay Interview results. When that day came, the managers trudged in with stacks of data that represented all inputs from those beneath them, up to three levels down. Marvin had given them a form to complete that listed the core subjects of pay, schedules, career, and communication. But Marvin also included a column identifying employee comments that could best be addressed by the company and another column showing comments best solved by the immediate supervisor. Marvin kept score on a flip chart in front of the room, and the final count was supervisor 62 percent, company 38 percent.

Examples where supervisors could improve included the following:

- "Provide ongoing feedback on improvement areas rather than hold it until the performance appraisal, and use the feedback as reason for a below-average raise."

- "Tell us when the policies change on patient communications instead of correcting me after I've done something wrong without knowing the new rules."

- "Give clearer instructions for doing a new procedure, so I feel good about learning on the job rather than feel bad about doing something wrong."

Marvin then said to the group: "This is a great lesson learned. I wondered if we would all learn things about our management styles we could all do better. From what I can see, every supervisor got some healthy feedback and needs to grow from it. That is, everyone but me because none of you were open with me. So I've made a list of changes I'm going to make to my style, and here they are." Marvin then distributed a page on which he had printed a form for each supervisor, top to bottom, to pledge management style changes to their team. Marvin's form included his changes, and he read them aloud and concluded, "Now you have one more chance for input ... but actually you can always give me input. Are these the changes I need to make?"

After reaching agreement, the management team members presented their own management changes to their teams. Each required some discussion and negotiation, but ultimately every manager and supervisor throughout Happy Endings reached agreement with their teams on daily supervisory improvements. They shared these improvement lists with their managers too, so their managers could support them ... and check on their progress.

Marvin now felt like a savvy retention leader. As the weeks went by, he reviewed each manager's Stay Interview results for ideas he could convert into company-wide programs. After much consideration, he chose only three and left the rest alone. He told the management team that he thought this new approach had placed more work on the managers and supervisors and that he did not want to burden them with implementing more than a few new programs. But Marvin knew his real reason: he wanted to test whether changes the supervisors made to their styles would raise next year's scores without improving company policies or programs.

Marvin's Stay Interview Strengths	Marvin's Stay Interview Shortcomings

Now that you have read and analyzed each of the scenarios, please rank-order them from *best to worst*. *Best* should be awarded to the manager who in your opinion did the most outstanding job with the scenario provided, compared to his or her peer managers in the other scenarios. *Worst* should be assigned to the manager who you believe handled his or her situation worse than the rest. For the best performance, place the number "1" after that scenario's description, and place a "7" next to the worst performance. Once you have chosen your best and worst, fill in the others in their appropriate places in Table 7.1.

Table 7.1		
Scenario	**Description**	**Rank**
#1	We Call During Dinner ... where Maria gave John more feedback than he could have ever imagined	
#2	Tipping Cows ... during which Billie managed Brenda through her technology fears and schedule wishes	
#3	RENRON Consulting ... where Charles fretted the worst for his company and his career choice	
#4	Parts-Is-Parts ... as we saw James throw a curve at Robert through a missing tooth	
#5	Burning Bridges ... where Shirley gave Paul direction about his career	
#6	Rump Roast ... during which Lester positioned himself for a transfer or promotion	
#7	Happy Endings ... where Marvin took a fresh approach to improving survey results	

Now that you have scored the scenarios, I invite you to compare your rank orders to those of others who have played the Stay Interview Game at http://www.C-SuiteAnalytics.com. You can also compare your rank orders to mine and read my reasons for each decision by clicking on "Solutions" and then on "Stay Interviews."

Chapter 8 | True Stories of Stay Interviews at Work

ollowing are five very effective examples of clients we have worked with who leveraged the full power of Stay Interviews to improve engagement and retention. These examples cover a wide variety of industries and circumstances.

Burcham Hills Retirement Community: A Life-Changing Event

Imagine for a moment that you were Joan Holda, HR director of Burcham Hills Retirement Community in East Lansing, Michigan. Joan saw the light regarding the power of Stay Interviews and trained her managers to conduct them. Sitting in the room was Joan's manager, Executive Director Pam Ditri, and Pam had already decided to conduct her first Stay Interview with Joan. This had the look of the student teaching the teacher, leading to an artificial experience for both Joan and Pam, where they would just go through the motions. But the outcome had a profound impact on Joan's life.

Joan had been with Burcham Hills for eight years, and her husband had just retired. As her manager, Pam understood the psychological impact of one spouse seeing the other stay home in the morning. On the one hand, she valued Joan and wanted the best for her, but selfishly *she valued Joan so much that she wanted her to stay.*

During their meeting, Joan told Pam that she stayed because she felt valued and knew she made a difference. After more discussion, Pam asked Joan what it would take for Joan to stay longer, to continue her contributions rather than follow her husband into retirement. She specifically invited Joan to talk with her when Joan wanted more flexible hours or new challenges because Pam was willing to evaluate ideas to make it work. That night Joan told her husband about the meeting, which caused them both to think about their futures with one new piece of information, that Pam was open to new thinking. Joan would continue to work full time for now.

While this exchange seems like the logical next step when a valued employee's spouse retires, many executives would have instead bypassed the topic rather than stir up Joan's thinking about retiring, too. But Pam addressed the issue head-on to continue to retain Joan even though she hoped she would not lose Joan. As Joan said later, the result was not just about retention but also about increasing her engagement: "I went home that night with incredible feelings of being appreciated, and my trust in Pam was never higher."

While Joan was benefitting from her Stay Interview with Pam, others throughout Burcham Hills were benefitting, too. Since implementing Stay Interviews and other retention tactics, nurse turnover has decreased by 72 percent and every newly-hired nurse has stayed for at least the targeted early hire period of 180 days.

Florida Hospital Zephyrhills: Connecting the Dots with Strategic Issues

Zephyrhills, Florida, refers to itself as the "City of Pure Water."[1] The town is located 34 miles northeast of Tampa and is the home of Florida Hospital Zephyrhills, a major employer and economic driver of the community. While the town's population is just 12,570,[2] the hospital's strong reputation for quality makes it a magnet for employees to commute each day from Tampa out to the country.

CEO Doug Duffield employs every smart idea he knows to deepen employee engagement and retention because health care talent is hard to find. When Doug and I first talked about Stay Interviews, he immediately connected the dots between these one-on-one verbal events and the hospital's two annual employee surveys, one for engagement and one for safety. The result was our designing a customized Stay Interview that addressed all pertinent concerns.

Doug and his team first studied the most recent engagement and safety survey results in order to identify areas that would most benefit from open discussions. Doug intuitively understood that the best solutions to these issues would be implemented at the department level or between individual supervisors and employees. The number of final Stay Interview questions was less than 10 and included core questions about reasons for staying and leaving as well as those deduced from the engagement and safety surveys.

We then trained all managers and supervisors, starting with Doug, to provide them with skills training and the customized scripted questions, so significant areas from all corners of the hospital were addressed.

Employee turnover at Florida Hospital Zephyrhills decreased by 37 percent. More importantly, nurse turnover decreased by 70 percent and nurses are the most expensive health care professionals for hospitals to replace. Stay Interviews played a major role in these improvements.

Advanced Technology Services: Merging Stay Interviews with Retention Risk

Known in the industry as ATS, this smart company provides outsourced maintenance work to factories; hence, its positioning statement is "We Make Factories Run Better."[3] ATS is headquartered in Peoria, Illinois, and employees work across the United States and in some international locations. The continued growth of ATS requires hiring and retaining technical employees who like to get their hands dirty. Top management realizes this group is dwindling.

One critical engagement and retention strategy is to build employees' skills. The ATS Cultural Commitment includes eight core statements the company lives by, including "Develop People," which underscores this primary value to better employees through their development.

Managers are required to design customized development plans with each employee and are held accountable for seeing the plans through. In the past, some managers complained that whereas some employees were eager to learn and advance, others were disinterested in any additional work activities and "just wanted to come to work and go home."

The solution to improving *retention, engagement,* and *development* was to provide a combination tool to managers that included both developmental examples and Stay Interview questions. This tool would not only address development but also shine light on any overlooked company activity that made ATS anything but a perfect place to work.

The initial step was to gather supervisor and employee subject matter experts who identified core competencies for both beginners and those employees who had moved on to greater responsibilities. Each of these subject matter experts then volunteered to take one of the resulting competencies and script activities supervisors could recommend to their employees to develop that competency. The subject matter experts went one step further, though, as they designed developmental activities for each competency that could be delivered either on the job, through feedback, or via company training programs, as suggested earlier in Chapter 5.

The resulting development meeting guide was combined with Stay Interview questions about reasons employees stayed and why they might leave. ATS top management asked each manager and supervisor to conduct these sessions annually and in most cases six months after performance appraisals. Follow-up sessions were scheduled as needed.

Working together, our team and savvy ATS executives added one more step. After each manager conducted a Stay Interview with a member of their teams, the manager entered that employee's level of "retention risk" into a confidential database. The retention risk indicator was deliberately simple ... "green" indicated the employee will stay for the foreseeable future, "yellow" indicated a concern, and "red" indicated a serious issue related to retention. The color-coding could be based on issues from either the employee or the manager. For each "yellow" and "red" indication, the manager entered an action plan to retain that employee, or if appropriate to initiate progressive discipline when the issue connected to performance.

The retention risk coding addressed several key retention issues. Executives and HR professionals were now able to see on their screens the broad-based talent retention issues by site, by job, by supervisor, and for the entire organization. Supervisors became more focused on retention because they had to declare a specific degree of risk for each employee. And next-up managers had a new tool for driving home retention accountability by linking subordinate supervisors' coding to actual retention trends. For example, when newly-hired employees were coded red and they eventually quit, managers would ask subordinate supervisors what lessons they learned from hiring that employee. Or when continuing employees quit after being consistently coded green, managers would ask subordinate supervisors what signals they missed by asking, "What wasn't that employee telling you? How can you improve your Stay Interview meetings so employees are more open?"

Some organizations have begun building predictive databases for retention based on past turnover data and marketplace trends. *The red/yellow/green method is better because it involves managers being responsible for their teams* rather than by relying on HR professionals to study data in isolation from the real issues across their companies.

Jim Hefti is ATS's top HR executive, and he reflects on the program this way:

> In the past we asked our onsite managers to meet with employees to help with development, but we came up short on giving them the tools they needed to be successful. Now managers not only address development with concrete ideas, but they are asking their employees about issues that are even more fundamental: "What makes you stay and what could cause you to leave?" Managers know they are in charge of their talent and we are giving them a great tool to enhance their success.[4]

A Purposed Transition: Retaining Nonprofit Boards

Kimberly Benjamin is executive director of A Purposed Transition, a nonprofit organization that helps people discover their purpose through career and entrepreneurial exploration. Kimberly used Stay Interviews to help retain board members and other volunteers with great results.

"We learned early on that retaining volunteers was essential to our delivering the services we promised, and building retention required relationships that were deep with trust," Kimberly says.[5] Conducting Stay Interviews was her solution. Kimberly found that volunteers participated for a wide range of reasons, so she could customize their roles to best suit both their interests and their skills. Since conducting Stay Interviews, the retention rate for board members and other volunteers has been 100 percent.

"Leaders need followers," Kimberly added. "Now I have a solid, steady team, and we can deliver on our promises to clients."

Novo 1: Saying It and Doing It

Mary Murcott is a friend, client, and CEO of NOVO 1, which is headquartered in Fort Worth, Texas. Mary is early in her CEO role and is committed to making NOVO 1 a *Fortune* 100 Best Place to Work. While many CEOs steer themselves toward this goal, Mary is especially ambitious because NOVO 1 is a multiple-site call center outsourcing company, and these organizations typically operate with greater than 100 percent employee turnover due to low profit margins and constant changes demanded by client companies. But NOVO 1 *feels* like a great place to work because of its stylish lobby area, stimulating colors everywhere, and positive energy that is generated by its employees.

I recently trained all managers at NOVO 1 to conduct Stay Interviews. Mary made concluding remarks after each session:

> I sat in the back of the room this morning and couldn't help but think about the ways we've been taught to think about our employees compared to how we think about our customers. We all know that "Customer Management 101" says never assume you know what your customers think so you need to ask them ... that silence from customers is never good news. So in restaurants and other businesses you see executives approach customers and ask their opinions of the services they just received.
>
> But this is different than how we treat employees! We build walls between us and them by asking opinions in anonymous surveys, which protect us from looking in their eyes and hearing their words. Maybe down deep we have a fear that they will ask for something, and we'll have to say no. Or maybe they'll ask for something that you think they deserve but don't have the authority to give them.
>
> We can't become a great company unless we ask, listen, and then consider every reasonable request. So my commitment to you is that our top team and I will listen to any idea you hear that you think has merit, either for all employees or just for one. You know that our most important goal is to run a profitable business for our shareholders, so we cannot say yes to every request. But our employees know this, too, and I don't think they will ask for impossible things.
>
> Let's declare that the game is over for sacred cows regarding pay, schedules, benefits, and all other subjects we usually run away from. Above all else, let's be courageous and

reasonable, and I am certain our employees will reasonable too."[6]

Mary nailed the difference between how we view customer relationships and employee relationships. We assume customers have realistic expectations for the services we provide, but we approach employees differently, expecting that many will insist pay is not fair or career opportunities come up short. The result is that we duck their questions to avoid the discomfort of giving an answer that they will reject and maybe make us unpopular.

Imbedded in Mary's approach are two distinct solutions. The first is that we will stretch our thinking to invent and consider outcomes that we have not considered before. The second is that we will anticipate everyone's maturity to understand reasonable thinking when we have to say no.

Months after Mary had spoken these words, she and her team faced a strong test to continue to provide the service her clients deserved. Football fans recall the uncharacteristic winter storms that plagued the Dallas area in February 2011 in advance of Super Bowl XLV. These same storms created huge difficulties for NOVO 1 employees to get to work in nearby Fort Worth. To enable employees to weather these storms and at the same time to deliver exceptional customer service, NOVO 1 provided the following for employees:

- Complimentary hotel rooms
- Free shuttle service
- Free taxi service
- Breakfast served by the senior management team
- Daily catered lunches
- Day care service from 7 a.m. to 7 p.m.

- Hourly prize drawings for iPods, iPads, gift cards, and vacation days as an extra way to thank employees who braved the elements to serve clients and customers

These ideas were based on employee inputs, and Mary approached her team with the same openness she used when initiating the Stay Interview process. The "final score," as Mary called it, was hundreds of positive messages sent by employees for caring, for living the company values, and for enhancing the NOVO 1 culture. Clients were also appreciative as they understood the challenges all Dallas-area businesses faced as their inclement weather was a fixture on all media outlets due to the game.

You can choose your metaphor for Mary Murcott. She walks the talk, leads by example, and does what she says ... and is fearless about hearing any good idea her employees tell her that will make her company better. And her approach to implementing Stay Interviews helped NOVO1 reduce employee turnover by 20 percent.

**

These true stories highlight the value of creative thinking, process integration, and leadership that is both open-minded and courageous. All were transformative events in their companies that lead to engagement and retention gaining deeper, thicker roots.

Chapter 9 | 'I've Burned the Ships'

In 1519, Spanish Capitan Hernando Cortes landed his crew at the shores of Mexico in a village named Vera Cruz. Historical accounts lead me to think none of us would refer to Cortes as a highly sensitive, caring guy but rather as one who set out to achieve his capitalistic goals at any cost. These same historical documents indicate that Cortes solved several management problems by burning his crews' ships so they could never go home again.[1]

As we bring our time together to a close, let us consider a few of the predicaments HR managers sometimes face when working with managers who see any form of people-management work as "HR work." These are managers ... and executives ... who may say any of the following when you introduce the Stay Interview concept:

- "How much time will this take? Our managers have more valuable things to do and are already stretched for time."

- "This is HR's work. Why don't you interview some employees in a focus group and then tell us what they think?"

- "We already do enough surveys, and we know what our employees think."

- "Our managers have too many direct reports. This could take months!"

- "Let's just give them more free food, and they'll all be happy."

OK, that last one is a stretch, but the others are not. My first job was working in personnel, and then over time we graduated to working in human resources. Looking back on perceptions, it seems one difference is that *personnel workers* were paper-pushers who listened to employees and advocated their concerns. HR *professionals* then became more involved with talent management, succession planning, and other activities that contributed to the company's strategic direction and also helped managers manage better.

Implementing Stay Interviews the proper way requires taking on all of the above-noted HR characteristics and more. Gone are the days when human resources conducted employee meetings as surrogate managers or absorbed unnerving stories during exit interviews which they keep to themselves for fear no one would take action if they shared them.

Knowledge *is* power, and action is power too. The main topic of this book is Stay Interviews and all the benefits they bring. If you take only one good idea away from this book besides implementing Stay Interviews, reread the section in Chapter 6 titled "Why Not Initiate a People-Management Balanced Scorecard?" Providing rightly directed and accurate information to your CEO about each manager's effectiveness with managing his or her people reinforces that it is the manager's job to manage his or her people, not yours.

In closing, think through the roles you play in your HR job and ask yourself which are about *personnel* and which are about *human resources*. Implementing Stay Interviews requires that HR provide support but that managers do the heavy lifting ... as they should. As you plan your implementation, "burn the ships" of those past surrogate leader roles you played, and do your best to never go back.

Endnotes

Chapter 1

1 Based on surveys of 800 participants at both SHRM's Annual Conference & Exposition and SHRM's Talent & Staffing Management Conference, 2010.

2 Watson Wyatt Worldwide, "Debunking the Myth of Employee Engagement: 2006/2007 WorkUSA Survey Report," 2006, http://au.hudson.com/documents/Debunking-the-Myths-of-Employee-Engagement.pdf.

3 Data presented from PricewaterhouseCooper's Saratoga Institute is from their report titled "Driving the Bottom Line: Improving Retention," 2006.

4 The reference to $25 billion to train replacements due to turnover is from Rudy Darsan, "The Real Cost of Turnover," *Kenexa Connection* newsletter, Volume 6, Issue 3.

5 The reference to turnover reducing U.S. corporate earnings and stock prices by 38 percent is from research by Sibson & Company as reported in "Employee Turnover Rates & Employee Retention Statistics," www.morebusiness.com, October 12, 2000.

Chapter 2

1 Richard P. Finnegan, *Rethinking Retention in Good Times and Bad: Breakthrough Ideas for Keeping Your Best Workers* (Boston, MA, and Alexandria, VA: Davies-Black and Society for Human Resource Management, 2010).

2 The reference to 14 percent of organizations setting retention goals at the first-line leader level is from "Employee Turnover Trends 2007" by TalentKeepers, 2007.

3 2009 Executive Retention Report: Engaged But Not Married: Restless Executives Poised To Pursue Opportunity Elsewhere, ExecuNet and Finnegan Mackenzie, The Retention Firm, p. 9, 2009.

Chapter 3

1 "Predicting Employee Engagement," DDI, (nd).

2 U.S. Merit Systems Protection Board, "The Power of Federal Employee Engagement," September 2008, www.mspb.gov/netsearch/viewdocs.aspx?docnumber=379024&version=379721&application=ACROBAT.

3 "Gallup Study: Feeling Good Matters in the Workplace," *Gallup Management Journal* news release, January 12, 2006, http://gmj.gallup.com/content/20770/Gallup-Study-Feeling-Good-Matters-in-the.aspx.

4 ASTD, "Learning's Role in Employee Engagement: Executive Summary of an ASTD Research Report," 2008, www.astd.org/NR/rdonlyres/AD2B2677-CC9D-4762-8683-C455826925AD/0/Engagement_ExecSumm.pdf.

5 The Saratoga Institute study is from "Hint: If You're a New Manager, It's Not All About You."

6 Marcus Buckingham and Curt Coffman, *First, Break All the Rules: What the World's Greatest Managers Do Differently* (New York: Simon & Schuster, 1999).

7 Tiffany M. Greene-Shortridge and Lisa Wager, "The Role of Person-Supervisor Fit on Employee Attitudes and Retention," *Kenexa HR Newsletter*, Volume 7, Issue 1.

8 Kathy Gurchiek, "Research Shows Five Ways to Gain Workers' Trust," www.shrm.org/hrnews, April 11, 2007.

9 "Loyalty in the Workplace," Walker Information, September 2007.

10 See the Great Place to Work Institute website at http://www.greatplacetowork.com/what_we_believe/trust.php

11 Adam Bryant, "Google's Quest to Build a Better Boss," *New York Times*, March 12, 2011.

Chapter 5

1 See Michael M. Lombardo and Robert W. Eichinger, For Your Improvement: *A Developmental Coaching Guide* (Lominger Limited, 1996).

Chapter 6

1 Fred Reichheld, "The Ultimate Question," (Cambridge, MA: Harvard Business School Press, 2006).

2 Finnegan, *Rethinking Retention in Good Times and Bad*, p. 70.

Chapter 8

1 See City of Zephyrhills, Florida, website at www.ci.zephyrhills.fl.us.

2 Linda Bowen, in interview with the author, March 10, 2011.

3 See www.advancedtech.com.

4 Author conversation with Jim Hefti, July 20, 2011.

5 Author conversation with Kimberly Benjamin, May 10, 2011.

6 Mary Murcott's address to her managers, August 19, 2010.

Chapter 9

1 Lisa Pinsley, "Loose Lips Burn Ships," *Fast Company*, June 30, 1997, www.fastcompany.com/magazine/09/cdu9.html.

Index

A

A Purposed Transition, 101
accountability, 13, 55, 100
accountable, 11, 13, 14, 52, 59,
60, 61, 98, *fig* 2.1
achievement orientation, 16
action plan(s), 5, 58, 99, *table* 1.2
adaptability, 16
Advanced Technology Services
(ATS), 98-100
    ATS Cultural Commitment,
    98
American Society for Training
and Development (ASTD), 18
attraction to work, 16

B

Bain & Company, 53
balanced scorecard, 60
benchmark(s), 1, 49, 56
    data, 3, 50
    scores, 58
Benjamin, Kimberly, 101
Bock, Laszlo, 23
Buckingham, Marcus, 19
Burcham Hills Retirement
Community, 95-6

C

climate surveys, 1
coach(es), 42, 55, 56
coaching, 17, 40, 45, 52
Coffman, Curt, 19
corporate earnings, 6
corporate success, 7
co-worker relations, 16
crowdsourcing, 39

D

dashboards, 60
detractors, 53
Development Dimensions International (DDI), 16
development, 11, 19, 42, 45, 48,
98, 100, fig 3.2
    meeting, 99
    plan(s), 32, 44, 45, 58, 98
developmental
    activities, 99
    opportunities, 44
    tools, 41
disengagement, 6
Ditri, Pam, 95-6
Duffield, Doug, 97

E

Eichinger, Robert, 45
emotional maturity, 16
employee satisfaction, 57
employee survey(s), 2, 3, 4, 35, 49, 50, 51, 56-9, 60, 97, table 2.1,
　action form, 58
　results, 35, 57, 88
　scores, 59, 60
employees' opinions, 1-2, 4, 19
engagement characteristics, 16
engagement surveys, 1, 49
engagement-building skills, 18
ExecuNet, 13
executive survey(s), table 5.2
exit interview(s), 54, 55, 106
exit survey(s), 1, 2, 3, 11, 49, 50-6, 57, table 1.1
　data, 50, 52
　process, 51
　vendors, 51

E

feedback, 17, 22, 45, 87, 91, 99
Feeling Good Matters in the Workplace, 18
First, Break All the Rules, 19
first-line supervisors, 9, 23, 28, 40
flextime, 44
Florida Hospital Flagler, 38
Florida Hospital Zephyrhills, 97
Fortune 100 Best Places to Work For, 22, 101

G

Gallup, 18, 19
Google, 23
Great Places to Work Institute, 22

H

Hefti, Jim, 100
high-performing

employees, 10
supervisors, 15
hiring, 11, 52, 98
Holda, Joan, 95-6
HR executives, 3, 34
HR managers, 9, 52, 55, 61, 105, table 1.1
HR professionals, 2, 9, 99, 100, 106
HR system, 52

J

jerk bosses, 11

K

Kenexa, 19

L

Leadership IQ, 22
Learning's Role in Employee Engagement, 18
leave reasons, 34, 50, 51, 52, 55, table 5.2
length of service, 30, 34, 43, 51, 52, 53, 60
Lombardo, Michael, 45
loyalty, 22, 39

M

marketplace trends, 100
mentoring, 44
morale, 15
Murcott, Mary, 101-04

N

net-promoter
　calculation, 58
　patterns, 53
　question, 57
　results, 53
　score(s), 53, 55, 60
new hires, 11, 12, 33, 55
NOVO 1, 101-04

O

operational metrics, 60

P

Panaralla, Sam, 54
Parker, Alyson, 39
passives, 53
people-management
    data, 60, 61
    situations, 78
    work, 105
performance appraisal(s), 13,
31, 81, 91, 99
    meetings, 29
performance, 22, 28, 29, 34, 43,
57, 60, 99
    data, 52
    discussion, 33, 65
    levels, 52, 53
    management, fig 2.2
    metrics, 59
    problems, 29
    rating scale, 52
    review(s), 33, 57
performers
    best, 4, 30
    high, 30, 32, 55
    low, 52
    top, 4, 5, 11, table 1.2
    worst, 5
positive disposition, 16
*The Power of Federal Employee
Engagement*, 17
productivity, 6, 14, 42, 47, 86
progressive discipline, 99
promoters, 53

R

recognition, 1, 11, 35, 58
Reichheld, Fred, 53, 54
retention
    accountability, 100
    goal(s), 11, 12, 13, 14, 25, 52
    plans, 14

processes, 13, *fig* 2.2
programs, 13, *fig* 2.2
rate(s), 21, 101
risk, 98, 99
solutions, 2, 3, 5, 11
strategy, 98
trends, 100
*Rethinking Retention in Good
Times and Bad*, 9, 54
Rethinking Retention Model®, 9,
11, 13, 14, 52, 61, *fig* 2.1
revenue per employee, 6, 60
role play, 37

S

Saratoga Institute, 6, 19
schedule flexibility, 43, 44, 48
self-efficacy, 16
stay interview
    data, 56
    feedback, 67
    improvement plans, 58
    meeting(s), 48, 65, 66, 100
    performance, 28
    process, 33, 36, 81, 104
    questions, 49, 50, 57, 90, 97,
    98, 99
    rollout, 39
    solutions, 48
stay plan(s), 5, 27, 32, 34, 35, 37,
44, 45, 47, 48
    individual, 5, 35
stay reasons, 34, *table* 5.2
stock prices, 6
succession planning, 106

T

talent, 52, 88
    management, 13, 106
    retention, 99-100
telecommuting, 28
training, 11, 12, 21, 31, 32, 34,
40, 42, 51, 52, 64, 82, 97
    cross-training, 44

trust, 11, 14, 21, 22, 23, 26, 35, 36, *fig* 2.1
turnover, 6, 9, 10, 14, 19, 21, 30, 33, 52, 55, 60, 61, 64, 89, 96, 101, 104, *fig* 2.1
    cost(s), 6, 10, 11, 12, *fig* 2.1
    data, 30, 100
    high-turnover industries, 6
    high-turnover managers, 52
    information, 35
    involuntary, 52
    problem, 19
    surge, 11
    voluntary, 52

U
U.S. Merit Systems Protection Board, 17

V
voluntary resignations, 50

W
Walker Information, 22
Watson Wyatt, 6
work effectiveness, 16
work style flexibility, 12
work/life balance, 12, 46, *table* 5.2
workplace demographics, 10
workplace flexibility, 43

Interested in Learning More About Stay Interviews?

Would reporting engagement and retention in actual dollars cause your executives to take stronger actions?

We have tools to help you implement every idea you've read in this book.

Our company, C-Suite Analytics, offers the following fresh-thinking solutions:

- More effective engagement and exit surveys
- Simple process for predicting employees' retention risk
- Employee retention certification online learning program
- And most importantly, a **Performance GPS Dashboard** for the optimum balance between financial metrics, customer metrics, and people metrics that report each manager's performance against engagement and

retention goals and the actual dollar cost of their performance.

For more information, please visit www.C-SuiteAnalytics.com or e-mail me at DFinnegan@C-SuiteAnalytics.com

About the Author

Dick Finnegan has been cited by *BusinessWeek, Chief Executive Magazine,* and *Consulting Magazine* as a leading thinker on employee retention.

Dick is the CEO of C-Suite Analytics (www.C-SuiteAnalytics.com), which helps organizations engage and retain their employees. He is also the author of *Rethinking Retention in Good Times and Bad* (Davies-Black/SHRM, 2010), which details the best strategic approach to cutting turnover with specific, research-based tactics that work.

His U.S. clients have included Sprint, Hilton, The Hartford, GE, and Johnson & Johnson, as well as the CIA. His international work has spanned 6 continents and includes working with Siberian banks as well as African gold mines where he went 3 kilometers deep to learn why employees stay and leave. He also partners with the Chinese HR Excellence Center to conduct employee retention programs across China.

Dick is a featured speaker for SHRM, ICMI, and other organizations. He holds bachelors and graduate degrees from The Pennsylvania State University and lives in Orlando, Florida, where the *Orlando Sentinel* newspaper published an editorial recognizing him for his extensive donations of professional services to non-profit organizations.

Additional SHRM-Published Books

101 Sample Write-Ups for Documenting Employee Performance Problems: A Guide to Progressive Discipline & Termination
By Paul Falcone

Assessing External Job Candidates
By Jean M. Phillips and Stanley M. Gully

Assessing Internal Job Candidates
By Jean M. Phillips and Stanley M. Gully

Business-Focused HR: 11 Processes to Drive Results
By Scott P. Mondore, Shane S. Douthitt, and Marisa A. Carson

Business Literacy Survival Guide for HR Professionals
By Regan W. Garey

The Chief HR Officer: Defining the New Role of Human Resource Leaders

Edited by Patrick M. Wright, John W. Boudreau, David A. Pace, Elizabeth "Libby" Sartain, Paul McKinnon, and Richard L. Antoine

The Cultural Fit Factor: Creating an Employment Brand That Attracts, Retains, and Repels the Right Employees

By Lizz Pellet

The Essential Guide to Federal Employment Laws

By Lisa Guerin and Amy DelPo

From Hello to Goodbye: Proactive Tips for Maintaining Positive Employee Relations

By Christine V. Walters

Got a Minute? The 9 Lessons Every HR Professional Must Learn to Be Successful

By Dale J. Dwyer and Sheri A. Caldwell

HR Competencies: Mastery at the Intersection of People and Business

By Dave Ulrich, Wayne Brockbank, Dani Johnson, Kurt Sandholtz, and Jon Younger

Human Resource Essentials: Your Guide to Starting and Running the HR Function

By Lin Grensing-Pophal

Leading with Your Heart: Diversity and *Ganas* for Inspired Inclusion

By Cari M. Dominguez and Jude Sotherlund

The Legal Context of Staffing

By Jean M. Phillips and Stanley M. Gully

The Manager's Guide to HR: Hiring, Firing, Performance Evaluations, Documentation, Benefits, and Everything Else You Need to Know

By Max Muller

Managing Diversity: A Complete Desk Reference & Planning Guide

By Lee Gardenswartz and Anita Rowe

Performance Appraisal Source Book

By Mike Deblieux

Proving the Value of HR: How and Why to Measure ROI

By Jack J. Phillips and Patricia Pulliam Phillips

Staffing Forecasting and Planning

By Jean M. Phillips and Stanley M. Gully

Staffing to Support Business Strategy

By Jean M. Phillips and Stanley M. Gully

Stop Bullying at Work: Strategies and Tools for HR and Legal Professionals

By Teresa A. Daniel

EXECUNET

FIRST BREAK ALL THE RULES